MICROSOFT CERTIFIED SYSTEMS ENGINEER

# MCSE Windows® XP Professional Lab Manual, Student Edition

Catherine Creary

**McGraw-Hill**/Osborne

New York   Chicago   San Francisco   Lisbon   London   Madrid
Mexico City   Milan   New Delhi   San Juan   Seoul   Singapore   Sydney   Toronto

**McGraw-Hill/Osborne**
2600 Tenth Street
Berkeley, California 94710
U.S.A.

To arrange bulk purchase discounts for sales promotions, premiums, or fund-raisers, please contact **McGraw-Hill**/Osborne at the above address. For information on translations or book distributors outside the U.S.A., please see the International Contact Information page immediately following the index of this book.

**MCSE Windows® XP Professional Lab Manual, Student Edition**

1234567890 CUS CUS 0198765432

ISBN 0-07-222512-2

| | | |
|---|---|---|
| **Publisher**<br>Brandon A. Nordin | **Senior Project Editor**<br>Betsy Manini | **Production and Editorial Services**<br>Anzai! Inc. |
| **Vice President & Associate Publisher**<br>Scott Rogers | **Acquisitions Coordinator**<br>Athena Honore | **Series Designer**<br>Roberta Steele |
| **Acquisitions Editor**<br>Chris Johnson | **Technical Editor**<br>Brian Carroll | |

This book was composed with Corel VENTURA™ Publisher.

**To Brian and Greg**—What's mine is yours.

**To Dean**—You are my sunshine.

**Catherine Creary** is an independent technical trainer, entrepreneur, and author. She currently holds a Bachelor of Education, MCT, MCSE, and MCDBA. Catherine has more than 12 years of experience in the field of education. She is the author of *Network+ All-in-One Lab Manual* (Osborne/McGraw-Hill, 2002), numerous training courses (Digital Think), and an Exchange 2000 column (www.OutlookExchange.com). She is also the author of several articles regarding cross-border employment for IT personnel. She has extensive experience in computer training, including development of adult education computer courses and curriculum design.

# CONTENTS

# ACKNOWLEDGMENTS

Thanks first and foremost to Chris Johnson, Athena Honore, and all the others at McGraw-Hill/Osborne who worked hard at putting this book together. Also, thanks to Brian Carroll for his invaluable technical edits.

Thanks to my agent Neil Salkind at Studio B Productions Ltd. (www.studiob.com), Krystin Pickens, Jessica Richards, and all the staff at Studio B.

Thanks to Bill Cope for providing me with the goods. Thanks to Ken Symes, Letham Burns, and Mitch Tulloch (www.mtit.com) for the tech talk.

And finally, thanks to Ann Fothergill-Brown, Tom Anzai, Allan Shearer, and Linda Shearer for their editorial and production assistance.

# INTRODUCTION

Welcome to the *MCSE Windows XP Professional Lab Manual*. This lab manual is meant to complement the *MCSE Windows XP Professional Study Guide* (Exam 70-270). Skills needed to deploy and manage Windows XP Professional components are reinforced with real-world lab exercises for each of the certification objectives. A prerequisite for successfully accomplishing the intended learning outcomes of this lab manual is an exposure to Windows XP Professional.

Each chapter includes a chapter introduction, a materials list, and setup instructions for each lab, as well as the lab exercises. The labs themselves include hands-on activities, and administration and troubleshooting questions. The labs not only prepare you for the Microsoft Windows XP Professional (70-270) exam but also prepare you for possible real-life scenarios that you may encounter with Windows XP Professional.

Each chapter also has five lab analysis questions and a key term quiz. Those exercises allow you to demonstrate your knowledge of the material covered in the chapter.

Finally, the chapter concludes with a brief summary of the key points. Step-by-step solutions to the labs are provided at the end of each chapter.

**In This Lab Manual**  This lab manual provides the necessary exposure and training for the tasks of installing, configuring, managing, monitoring, and troubleshooting a Windows XP Professional computer. Topics that are covered include:

- Attended and unattended installations
- Local computer and security policies
- User and hardware profiles
- Modems, USB devices, and wireless links
- Disk quotas and management
- Printers and faxes

- Resource administration
- Virtual private networks
- Remote desktop and remote assistance
- Internet connection firewall
- Encrypting file system (EFS)
- Optimizing system performance

After completing this lab manual, you will have a better understanding of the Windows XP Professional infrastructure, and you will be capable of managing its daily operations.

## Lab Exercises

Understanding the theory behind networking and Windows XP Professional principles is important for a network administrator. But, can you transfer this knowledge to a system situation? Each exercise allows you to apply and practice a particular concept or skill in a real-world scenario.

**Case Studies**   Each certification objective is presented as a case study. The cases provide a conceptual opportunity to apply your newly developed knowledge.

**Learning Objectives**   Working hand-in-hand with the study guide, this manual's main objective is to help you pass the certification exam. Its second objective is to help you develop critical thinking. In networking, not all installations, re-installations, or network and system problems present themselves in the same fashion every time. To this end you need to be able to analyze, to consider your options and the result of each option, to select and implement that option. If it works, great; if it doesn't, you start over again.

**Lab Materials and Setup**   If you are to fully accomplish each lab, it is necessary that the hardware and software requirements below be met. If meeting the requirements is not possible, then read through the steps and become familiar with the procedures as best you can.

- Two (2) Windows XP Professional computers: 64MB RAM, Pentium 133 MHz or higher
  - VGA monitor or better
  - Mouse or other pointing device
  - 12× CD-ROM or faster
  - One or more hard drives with a minimum of 4GB free space
  - Network card with either a BNC (coaxial cable) or cat5 connection
  - Dial-up or LAN connection
- Windows 2000 Server or Advanced Server computer
  - 128MB of RAM, Pentium 133 MHz or higher
  - VGA monitor or better
  - Mouse or other pointing device
  - 12× CD-ROM or faster
  - One or more hard drives with a minimum of 4GB free space
  - Network card with either a BNC (coaxial cable) or cat5 connection
- The computers can be connected using a small network hub.

**Getting Down-to-Business**    The hands-on portion of each lab proceeds step-by-step, not click-by-click. You receive explanations and instructions that walk you through each task relevant to the certification exam.

## Lab Analysis Test

The lab analysis test contains short-to-medium-answer questions that quickly assess your comprehension of what you've learned in the study guide and tbe labs in the chapter. The answers should be in your own words, showing that you've synthesized the information and that you have a comprehensive understanding of the key concepts.

## Key Term Quiz

The key term quiz highlights technical words that you should be able to recognize. Knowing their definitions and purpose will help you in the exam and on the job.

## Solutions

Each chapter provides solutions for the lab exercises, the lab analysis test, and the key term quiz. You can compare your lab procedures, or answer, or definition, with the correct lab procedures, or answer, or definition. Individuals that may be very familiar with Windows XP Professional will find that, in certain parts of the lab exercises, there is more than one way to accomplish the step. The end result, and the understanding of the process required to reach that end result is the main objective.

MICROSOFT CERTIFIED SYSTEMS ENGINEER

# Introduction to Microsoft Windows XP Professional

## LAB EXERCISES

W elcome to the *MCSE Windows XP Professional Lab Manual!* This book provides real-life scenarios similar to those that you, the reader, may encounter in the future when dealing with the Windows XP Professional operating system. It also prepares you to write Microsoft exam 70-270.

This book is part of the McGraw-Hill/Osborne MCSE series, which includes the *MCSE Windows XP Professional Study Guide Exam 70-270,* the textbook that teaches the concepts and terms you need to know to complete the labs presented here. Both books are organized in 13 chapters, the lab manual chapters mapping to the chapters of the study guide.

In this manual, you learn by practice, applying what the *MCSE Windows XP Professional Study Guide Exam 70-270* introduced using network scenarios. You can use your own computer system to simulate real-life scenarios. This book has been designed for readers in either a home network or a classroom environment. The sample screens and other illustrations also make this book an excellent learning tool for readers who may not have the hardware needed to accomplish all of the tasks on their own systems.

Each chapter presents step-by-step, hands-on labs that teach you how to install and administer Windows XP Professional. It also includes design labs in which you plan for future installations and administration. At most, the labs require an NT or Windows 9*x* personal computer, the Windows XP Professional CD, and a Windows 2000 Server with Domain Name Service (DNS), Dynamic Host Configuration Protocol (DHCP), and Active Directory (AD) installed. Every chapter in the book also includes a lab analysis test and a key term quiz. If you are preparing for Microsoft exam 70-270, you will find this book—with its active approach to the hands-on tasks that you will encounter during the exam and on the job—a valuable resource for understanding the concepts and terminology.

This chapter's lab, your first, is designed to prepare you for your future with the Windows XP Professional operating system.

## LAB EXERCISE 1.01

# Introducing Windows XP Professional

**30 Minutes**

Lynn is considering upgrading her home office computers from Windows 98 to Windows XP Professional. She wants all of her home computers to be connected to the Internet through one simple network connection. She does not want to have to read and research a thick manual to understand how to accomplish tasks on the operating system. She would like a user-friendly design. She has heard about the advanced features of Windows XP Professional and has asked your help in determining whether an upgrade will meet her needs.

## Learning Objectives

In this lab, you plan an installation of several Windows XP Professional computers in a small office. At the end of the lab, you'll be able to

- Identify the new design features of Windows XP Professional.
- Identify the new tools and networking features of Windows XP Professional.

## Lab Materials and Setup

The materials you need for this lab are

- Pencil and paper
- Computer with Windows XP Professional operating system (optional)

## Getting Down to Business

**Step 1.**   In the space provided, briefly list the two user interface designs available from Windows XP Professional.

_____

_____

**Step 2.**   In the space provided, briefly list the new management tools available with Windows XP Professional.

_____

_____

**Step 3.**   In the space provided, briefly list and define the networking features of Windows XP Professional.

_____

_____

**Step 4.**   What features of Windows XP Professional will satisfy Lynn's home office needs?

_____

_____

## LAB WRAP-UP

The Windows XP Professional operating system provides its users with a new interface, several new tools, and new hardware and networking features. You should now be aware of the new features and tools available in the Windows XP interface. The next chapter examines the process of completing an attended installation of Windows XP Professional.

# LAB SOLUTIONS FOR CHAPTER 1

In this section, you'll find the solutions to your first lab exercise.

## Lab Solution 1.01

To set up Lynn's efficient, single network connection to the Internet, you should have considered the operating system features described here.

**Step 1.** Windows XP Professional introduces a colorful new design for the user interface. Additionally, on the desktop, you see only the Recycle Bin, leaving more space for applications or shortcuts. The Start menu is completely configurable. Lynn can set up more items and as many expandable menus as she chooses to configure. By accessing the Start menu and Taskbar property sheets, she can configure the way the system looks and which items appear on the Start menu. She can also arrange for items to remain hidden. The "classic" Start menu view is also available. Windows XP also offers desktop themes and a graphical, streamlined view through the system. Folders are very easy to use; they even suggest tasks to users.

**Step 2.** The common management tools that are found in Windows XP Professional include the Performance and the Computer Management consoles, the Local Users and Groups setups, shared folders, an event viewer, a device manager, disk management, and the Microsoft Management Console (MMC).

**Step 3.** These networking features are available in Windows XP Professional:

- Windows XP Professional can automatically assign itself an IP address and auto-configure TCP/IP settings.

- Windows XP Professional is fully compatible with Windows 2000 networking and can function with DHCP and DNS network servers.

- You can make changes to the IP configuration of Windows XP Professional without having to reboot.

- Windows XP Professional can more easily detect network media and can use universal Plug and Play (PNP) to automatically install the drivers required for the media.

■ Windows XP Professional can be used as a dialup server and a web server, and it can be used to establish virtual private networks.

■ Home and small-office users can take advantage of Internet connection sharing, in which one computer is connected to the Internet and other network computers can use the Internet via that connection.

■ You can use remote assistance to help users across the Internet, and you can use remote desktop to run a computer remotely.

■ The new Internet connection firewall (ICF) is designed to work with Internet connection sharing. It helps home and small-office users protect their computers and networks from Internet attacks.

**Step 4.**   Lynn wants to have all of her home computers connected to the Internet through one simple network connection. The Internet connection sharing feature of Windows XP Professional satisfies that need. The user-friendly design and the tasks that Windows XP Professional suggests for her will satisfy Lynn's desire for a user-friendly operating system.

MICROSOFT CERTIFIED SYSTEMS ENGINEER

# 2

# Performing an Attended Installation of Windows XP Professional

## LAB EXERCISES

T his chapter examines the factors that you need to consider before attempting a Windows XP Professional installation. It also looks at the various methods of installing Windows XP Professional. You will be presented with several real-world scenarios and asked to determine which method of installation suits the scenario: installing from a CD-ROM, a network share, or the Winnt32.exe setup program. You will also need to determine whether it is best to upgrade an operating system or to perform a clean installation of Windows XP Professional. Finally, you will use your troubleshooting skills and knowledge to resolve and restore a failed Windows XP Professional installation.

The labs that follow are designed to prepare you to plan, modify, and troubleshoot a Windows XP Professional installation.

**LAB EXERCISE 2.01**

# Planning a Windows XP Professional Installation

**45 Minutes**

Aidan Enterprises is a small music publishing company that is considering upgrading all of its client computers to Windows XP Professional. The managers have hired you to help them determine the best plan for upgrading the client computers.

The current network comprises one Windows 2000 server and fifteen Windows client computers. Ten of the client computers are running Windows 98. Those computers have 500 MHz processors and 32MB RAM. The remaining five client computers are running Windows NT 4.0 Workstation. They have 600 MHz processors and 128MB RAM. All client computers have 4GB hard drives with a minimum of 2GB free space on each drive. Aidan Enterprises wants to maintain the existing music software applications and settings on each client computer. They don't know whether the music software applications are compatible with Windows XP Professional. Because there are performance problems with the server, they also want to avoid having their server host the Windows XP Professional installation files.

## Learning Objectives

In this lab, you plan the installation of several Windows XP Professional computers in a small company. At the end of the lab, you'll be able to

- Recognize and list the hardware and software requirements for installing Windows XP Professional.
- Determine the appropriate upgrade path for the Windows client computers.
- Suggest a method of installation that suits the company's needs.

## Lab Materials and Setup

The materials you need for this lab are

- Pencil and paper
- Access to the Internet

## Getting Down to Business

These steps guide you through the process of planning a Windows XP Professional installation.

**Step 1.**   On the lines that follow, list the minimum hardware requirements for installing Windows XP Professional on a computer. Do all of the company's client computers meet the minimum requirements? If not, what steps need to be taken before Windows XP Professional can be installed on all client computers?

_____

_____

**Step 2.**   The Windows XP Professional operating system makes two installation types available: clean install and upgrade. List the differences between those installation types. Which type of installation best suits the needs of Aidan Enterprises? Give reasons for your answer.

_____

_____

**Step 3.** Aidan Enterprises has indicated that they want to keep their existing music application software. What steps can you take to determine whether the software is compatible with Windows XP Professional? If the software is not compatible, can Windows XP Professional still be installed on the client computers? Give reasons for your answers.

_____

_____

*You may need to research on the Internet or using Windows XP help to discover the tools available for determining application compatibility.*

**Step 4.** Aidan Enterprises has indicated that they want to avoid using their server to host the installation files. What methods of installation are available for the client computers?

_____

_____

**LAB EXERCISE 2.02**

# Using Winnt32.exe to Modify a Windows XP Professional Setup

**60 Minutes**

Fransblow's Furniture has hired you to install Windows XP Professional on several of the company's client computers. You have chosen to set up a distribution server and to use the Winnt32.exe program to run the setup program from the client computers. You also plan to take advantage of the various switches that are available to modify the setup of Windows XP Professional on the client computers. Fransblow's Furniture has asked you to ensure that the Recovery Console is installed with the XP installation and also that the Windows XP Professional source files are copied to the hard disk of the server.

## Learning Objectives

In this lab, you use Winnt32.exe to modify a Windows XP Professional setup. At the end of the lab, you'll be able to

- Recognize the setup switches available to modify the Windows XP Professional installation.
- Use the Winnt32.exe program to install Windows XP Professional.

## Lab Materials and Setup

The materials you need for this lab are

- One PnP computer that meets the hardware and hardware compatibility list requirements for installing Windows XP Professional, and that has one of these operating systems installed: Windows 98, NT 4.0 Workstation, Windows Me, Windows 2000 Professional, or Windows XP Home
- One Windows XP Professional CD

## Getting Down to Business

These steps guide you through the process of using Winnt32.exe to modify a Windows XP Professional setup.

**Step 1.** Briefly define and compare the Winnt.exe and the Winnt32.exe programs.

_____

_____

**Step 2.** List and describe four setup switches that are available for use with the Winnt32.exe program.

_____

_____

**Step 3.** On the lines that follow, indicate the syntax for an installation of Windows XP Professional that would suit the needs of Fransblow's Furniture.

_____

_____

**Step 4.** Install Windows XP Professional on your computer using these steps:

1. With Windows running, insert the Windows XP Professional CD into the CD-ROM drive.

2. Owing to the autorun feature of the CD, a Windows XP Professional window may open. Close the window. Click Start, and select Run.

3. Type the following command, where D: is the CD-ROM drive letter:

   ```
   D:\i386\winnt32.exe /cmdcons
   ```

4. Follow the instructions on the screen to complete the Windows XP Professional setup.

**lab Hint** *In large environments such as Fransblow's Furniture, where many computers are configured with Windows XP Professional, post-installation product activation may or may not be necessary, depending on the licensing agreement between the corporation and Microsoft. For the purposes of this lab, you will not be activating the product.*

**Step 5.** What is the function of the /cmdcons switch? After you complete the setup of Windows XP Professional, verify that the Recovery Console is installed.

_____

_____

**lab Hint** *You may have to research the Windows XP web site to determine how to locate and run the Recovery Console.*

**LAB EXERCISE 2.03**

# Troubleshooting a Failed Windows XP Professional Installation

**30 Minutes**

Brian attempted to install Windows XP Professional on his home computer, but the installation failed at the Microsoft configuration screen. Brian rebooted his computer and the installation continued for a few short minutes. But the system then hung after completing the power-on self test (POST). Brian is asking your advice to help troubleshoot his installation problem.

## Learning Objectives

At the end of the lab, you'll be able to

- Recognize the causes of a failed Windows XP Professional installation.
- Analyze the setup log from a Windows XP installation.
- Recommend a solution for a small company's deployment of Windows XP Professional.

## Lab Materials and Setup

For this lab exercise, you'll need

- Pencil and paper
- A computer with Windows XP Professional successfully installed

## Getting Down to Business

These steps guide you through the process of troubleshooting a failed Windows XP Professional setup.

**Step 1.** What could be the cause of Brian's installation problem? Briefly give reasons for your answer.

_____

_____

**Step 2.** Where on a computer can you find clues about what may have caused a Windows XP Professional installation to fail? What type of information is available there?

_____

_____

**Step 3.** Locate the installation log on your personal computer, and list any failures in the space provided here.

_____

_____

**Step 4.** What changes can Brian make to his home computer to prevent further installation problems?

_____

_____

# LAB ANALYSIS TEST

1. How does Microsoft enforce the end-user license agreement of one CD per computer during a Windows XP Professional installation?

   _____

   _____

2. What is the purpose of the /checkupgradeonly command line switch?

   _____

   _____

3. If you are choosing to install Windows XP Professional in a dual-boot configuration, what must you consider in terms of choosing a file system?

   _____

   _____

4. Can the Windows NT 3.51 operating system be directly upgraded to Windows XP Professional? Give reasons for your answer.

   _____

   _____

5. What must you do before you install Windows XP Professional if you have antivirus software installed on your computer?

   _____

   _____

# KEY TERM QUIZ

Use the following vocabulary terms to complete the sentences below. Not all of the terms will be used.

- automatic updates
- distribution server
- dynamic updates
- File and Settings Transfer wizard
- hardware ID number
- product activation
- product key
- service pack
- slipstreaming
- softlifting
- Winnt32.exe
- Winnt.exe

1. To update files, to correct problems with the operating system, and to plug any security holes, a(n) _____ should be applied to the Windows XP Professional installation.

2. With _____ , Windows XP Professional can automatically check for and download Windows XP updates from Microsoft's web site.

3. _____ is a new feature from Microsoft that enforces the Windows XP license agreement and prevents one copy of the software from being installed on multiple computers.

4. _____ is the process of integrating a service pack with the installation image so that both are installed at the same time.

5. The _____ helps you to move your data files and personal settings from an old computer to a new one quickly and easily.

# LAB WRAP-UP

Windows XP Professional is an operating system that allows for many installation types, methods, and setup options. You should now be familiar with planning, executing, and troubleshooting an attended installation of Windows XP Professional. The next chapter examines the process of completing an unattended installation.

# LAB SOLUTIONS FOR CHAPTER 2

In this section, you'll find solutions to the lab exercises, lab analysis test, and key term quiz.

## Lab Solution 2.01

Your plans for installing Windows XP Professional at Aidan Enterprises should resemble those outlined here.

**Step 1.** The minimum hardware requirements for a Windows XP Professional installation are these: Pentium 233 MHz processor, 64MB RAM, 1.5GB free hard disk space, VGA monitor, Windows-compatible mouse, and Windows-compatible CD-ROM drive.

The Windows 98 client computers at Aidan Enterprises do not meet the minimum requirements of 64MB RAM. Additional RAM must be installed before Windows XP Professional can be installed on those computers.

**Step 2.** During an upgrade installation of Windows XP, the operating system installs in the same folder as the previous operating system, upgrading files and drivers as needed. A clean install of Windows XP installs the operating system in a different folder. Once the clean install is complete, all existing applications must be reinstalled.

Because Aidan Enterprises wants to maintain the existing music software applications, the best solution is to use the upgrade option. In that case, none of the existing applications need be reinstalled.

**Step 3.** To determine whether the existing application software is compatible with a new installation of Windows XP Professional, you can complete *one* of the following steps from the operating system:

- Click Start | Help | Support. Under Pick a Task, click Find Compatible Hardware and Software for Windows XP.

*or*

- Click Start | Help | Support. Type **program compatibility wizard** into the Search box. Click OK.

If the music software applications are not compatible with Windows XP Professional, the XP operating system can still be installed on a separate partition, creating a dual-boot configuration on the computer. The current operating system and applications remain on the initial partition, and the Windows XP Professional operating system and any additional XP-compatible applications can be installed on a new partition. Dual-boot is not an optimal solution for Aidan Enterprises, because most clients and administrators do not want to maintain two operating systems on one computer.

**Step 4.**    The installation methods available for Windows XP Professional include installing from a CD, setting up a distribution server and installing over the network, and using the Winnt32.exe program to run the installation with modified setup options.

Because Aidan Enterprises has determined that they want to avoid using the server to host the installation files, it is likely that they would avoid implementing the network installation method, which requires creating a distribution server and copying the contents of the Windows XP Professional CD to a shared folder. Another available installation method is to install each client computer from a CD. In a real-world scenario, that approach could take a great deal of time if several CDs were not available. Another option is to run the Winnt32.exe program. Using Winnt32.exe, Aidan Enterprises can modify setup options—for example, creating additional folders in which to place system files.

## Lab Solution 2.02

Your use of Winnt32.exe to modify a Windows XP Professional installation should resemble the approach outlined here.

**Step 1.**    The Winnt.exe program is used to perform a clean installation of Windows XP Professional on a drive that does not already have an operating system installed. You cannot use Winnt.exe to upgrade an existing version of Windows to Windows XP. The Winnt32.exe program is used to upgrade supported versions of Windows. It also handles a variety of setup switches.

**Step 2.**    Answers will vary. A complete list of supported command line switches can be found in Chapter 2 of the *MCSE Windows XP Professional Study Guide* by Curt Simmons (McGraw-Hill/Osborne, 2002) or at http://www.winsupersite.com/showcase/win2k_cmdline_setup.asp.

**Step 3.** The syntax for installing the Recovery Console and installation source files on the server is

```
Winnt32 /cmdcons /makelocalsource
```

**Step 4.** Answers will vary based on selections chosen during setup.

**Step 5.** The /cmdcons switch installs the Recovery Console as a startup option on a functioning computer. To run the Recovery Console, restart the computer and select the Recovery Console option from the list of available options.

## Lab Solution 2.03

Your approach to troubleshooting a failed Windows XP Professional installation should resemble those outlined here.

**Step 1.** Occasionally, during hardware detection and driver installation, a computer can lock up. The fact that Brian's computer hung may be a symptom that points to the cause of the installation failure. The failure was most likely caused by incompatible hardware, or hardware that did not meet the minimum hardware requirements.

**Step 2.** The setupact.log, found in the default C:\Winnt directory is a setup log that provides information on the events that took place during the installation of Windows XP Professional. The log lists the names of any files copied to the computer and the directories in which those files were installed. In the log, you may also see error messages indicating that a file was not deleted because it could not be found, or that a file failed to install properly. The log also indicates when files were not signed properly.

**Step 3.** Answers will vary. Figure 2-1 shows a sample setupact.log.

Viewing a typical
setupact.log

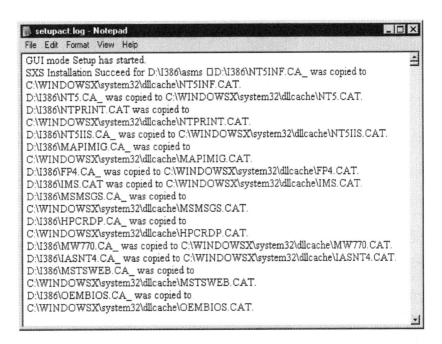

**Step 4.**    Brian can search through the setupact.log to determine the exact cause of his problem. He can then replace any incompatible hardware before reattempting to install Windows XP Professional.

## ANSWERS TO LAB ANALYSIS TEST

1. Microsoft XP Professional uses a new feature called Product Activation to enforce the client license agreement. The license agreement specifies that a given copy of Windows XP can be installed on one computer only. During installation, the Windows XP Professional product key is combined with a generated hardware identifier number to create a unique installation ID. That ID is then registered with Microsoft, and, upon activation of the product, the license agreement is enforced.

2. The /checkupgradeonly command line switch can be used with the Winnt32.exe program to check a computer for upgrade compatibility with Windows XP Professional. It allows the results of the check to be displayed on the screen, or saved to a file, or both.

3. When choosing to install Windows XP Professional in a dual-boot configuration, you must be aware that, if you choose to install Windows XP Professional on an NTFS partition, you may not be able to read the NTFS partition from the other operating system. Windows 95/98 and Me can read only FAT or FAT32 partitions. In such a scenario, you may therefore want to install Windows XP Professional on a partition formatted with the FAT32 file system.

4. The Windows NT 3.51 operating system cannot directly be upgraded to Windows XP Professional. You first need to upgrade to Windows NT 4.0 Workstation, and then to upgrade to Windows XP Professional.

5. Antivirus software should be disabled before Windows XP Professional is installed. Antivirus software will interfere with the installation because it works in the background, constantly checking for viruses.

## ANSWERS TO KEY TERM QUIZ

1. service pack
2. automatic updates
3. product activation
4. slipstreaming
5. File and Settings Transfer wizard

MICROSOFT CERTIFIED SYSTEMS ENGINEER

# 3

# Performing an Unattended Installation of Windows XP Professional

## LAB EXERCISES

U nattended installations can be implemented in one of two ways with Windows XP Professional—scripted or imaged. This chapter examines three company scenarios. Each scenario introduces a unique step in the process of an unattended installation, from preparing an answer file for a scripted installation, to using the system preparation (SysPrep) tool to prepare a computer for imaging.

Windows XP Professional also supports Remote Installation Services (RIS), a service that runs on Windows 2000 Server. You need RIS to deploy remote installations of Windows XP Professional. In this chapter, you'll also examine the process of creating a remote installation preparation (RIPrep) image for a Windows XP Professional installation.

Each lab is designed to help you better understand the procedures for implementing an unattended installation of Windows XP Professional.

**LAB EXERCISE 3.01**

# Preparing a Computer for an Unattended Installation of Windows XP Professional

**60 Minutes**

You have been hired by Bathurst Resources, a large industrial supply company, to deploy Windows XP Professional on 1500 client computers. The current network comprises 50 Windows 2000 Servers, 500 Windows 98 client computers, and 1000 Windows NT 4.0 Workstation computers. Management at Bathurst Resources want you to deploy a cost-effective solution in the shortest time possible. You choose to implement a scripted installation of Windows XP Professional, allowing yourself to view the pages of the Windows Setup wizard as the unattended installation progresses.

## Learning Objectives

In this lab, you plan an installation of several Windows XP Professional computers in a large company. At the end of the lab, you'll be able to

- List and define the tools used to prepare a computer for a scripted installation of Windows XP Professional.

- Create an answer file.
- Define the execution path for running the unattended installation for Bathurst Resources.

## Lab Materials and Setup

The materials you need for this lab are

- Pencil and paper
- One computer with a Windows operating system (98, Me, or NT 4.0 Workstation) installed
- Windows XP Professional CD
- File extraction software located on the computer's hard drive

## Getting Down to Business

In this lab, you apply the knowledge that you acquired in the *MCSE Windows XP Professional Study Guide* by Curt Simmons (McGraw-Hill/Osborne, 2002) for implementing an unattended scripted installation.

**Step 1.** List and define the tools used to prepare a computer for a scripted installation of Windows XP Professional.

_____

_____

**Step 2.** From the Windows XP Professional CD, extract the Setup Manager tool from the Deploy.cab file.

lab
ⓗint
*You can find the Deploy.cab file in the Tools folder on the Windows XP Professional CD. Refer to the **MCSE Windows XP Professional Study Guide** by Curt Simmons (McGraw-Hill/Osborne, 2002) for information on how to extract a file from a cabinet (.cab file).*

**Step 3.** Launch the Setup Manager tool and choose to create a new answer file for an unattended installation of the Windows XP Professional platform.

**Step 4.** Choose the level of user interaction that allows you to view, but not modify, the ongoing installation.

**Step 5.** Choose to create a new distribution folder shared as Distribution on the C: drive of your computer. Copy the setup files from the Windows XP Professional CD to the newly created folder.

**Step 6.** Customize the answer file settings for Bathurst Resources using the information shown here:

| Name | Bathurst Resources |
| --- | --- |
| Organization | Industrial Supply Co. |
| Colors | True color (32 bit) |
| Screen area | 800×600 |
| Refresh frequency | Use Windows default |
| Time zone | (GMT -04:00) Atlantic Time (Canada) |
| Product key | Enter the Product Key from your personal CD |
| Computer names | TestComputer |
| Administrator password | 200%@BRC (choose to have the password encrypted) |
| Networking components | Typical settings |
| Windows Server domain | Domain1 (Computer account: Administrator; Password: password) |

lab
ⓗint *Setup uses the data provided in the answer file to configure the automated setup of Windows XP Professional.*

**Step 7.** Accept the default name and location when saving the answer file. Windows XP Professional then begins to copy the files to the distribution folder.

**Step 8.** Once the answer file is created, what is the final step in implementing the unattended installation for Bathurst Resources client computers?

_____

_____

## LAB EXERCISE 3.02

# Performing a Remote Installation of Windows XP Professional

**90 Minutes**

Washburn Electronics is considering updating all of their client computers in Edinburgh and Glasgow from Windows NT 4.0 Workstation to Windows XP Professional. Their network consists of 800 computers distributed as shown here:

| London | 400 client computers |
|---|---|
| Edinburgh | 200 client computers |
| Glasgow | 200 client computers |

Management at Washburn want the client computer installation image to contain both the Windows XP Professional operating system and the Microsoft Excel application. They also want clients to be able to connect to a central server in London to begin the automatic installation of the image. They have asked you to implement an upgrade solution that will satisfy their requests.

## Learning Objectives

In this lab, you implement an automated remote installation of Windows XP Professional for a medium-sized company. At the end of the lab, you'll be able to

- Set up a RIS server
- Create a RIS boot disk
- Create a RIPrep image

## Lab Materials and Setup

The materials you need for the lab are

- Networked computer with Windows 2000 Server or Advanced Server operating system installed and an NTFS drive with 2GB free space.

■ Active Directory must be installed. Domain Name Service (DNS) and Dynamic Host Configuration Protocol (DHCP) must be active on your network.

■ Networked computer with Windows XP Professional operating system installed on a single disk with a single partition.

■ Blank formatted floppy disk.

## Getting Down to Business

This lab guides you in creating a RIS installation image. You will have to apply the knowledge that you acquired from the *MCSE Windows XP Professional Study Guide* by Curt Simmons (McGraw-Hill/Osborne, 2002) to complete the lab.

**Step 1.**   In the space provided, list the steps that will need to be completed at each location (London, Edinburgh, and Glasgow) to satisfy the requests made by Washburn Electronics.

_____

_____

**Step 2.**   On the Windows 2000 Server, install the RIS component and create the RemoteInstall folder on the NTFS partition. Allow the server to respond to known client requests automatically once setup is complete. Ensure that the server does not respond to unknown client requests.

**Step 3.**   In the space provided, indicate the steps necessary to authorize a RIS server in the Active Directory domain. What Windows 2000 security right must your user account possess to be able to authorize a RIS server?

_____

_____

**Step 4.**   To create a RIS boot disk for the computer, complete these steps:

1. On the Windows 2000 Server, log on as an administrator.

2. Click Start | Run, and type **RBFG.exe**, and click OK.

**lab**
**Hint**   *You can also access the utility via UNC path at \\servername\REMINST\ Admin\i386\rbfg.exe.*

3. The Remote Boot Disk Generator window opens.

4. Place a blank formatted floppy disk into the disk drive. Select the Create Disk button.

**Step 5.** From the Windows XP Professional computer, connect to the Windows 2000 server and run the RIPrep.exe program. Choose to copy the Windows XP Professional image to the RemoteInstall folder on the Windows 2000 server.

**lab**
**Ⓗint**

*The users at Washburn Electronics want an installation image that contains the Excel application as well as the XP Professional operating system. Before imaging takes place, Excel must be installed. Because of time and software restrictions, this lab omitted the installation of Excel.*

**LAB EXERCISE 3.03**

# Using SysPrep to Prepare a Windows XP Professional ImageSysPrep

**30 Minutes**

You have been hired by ThinkTech educational centers to prepare classroom setups for all Microsoft technical classes being taught by the centers. All student computers in the classrooms require identical installations of Windows XP Professional; however, each computer requires a unique security identifier.

## Learning Objectives

Although peripherals come in all shapes, sizes, and technologies, you can apply a standard set of procedures to the installation and configuration of peripherals. At the end of the lab, you'll be able to

■ Identify the steps that must be taken before the SysPrep tool can be used.

■ Identify the files associated with the SysPrep tool.

■ Define all steps required to complete a technical setup for the ThinkTech classroom.

## Lab Materials and Setup

For this lab exercise, you'll need a pencil and paper.

## Getting Down to Business

In the next few steps, you'll consider how to use SysPrep effectively for unattended installations of Windows XP Professional.

**Step 1.**   In the space provided, briefly describe the steps that must be completed on any computer before the SysPrep tool can be used.

_____

_____

**Step 2.**   Four components are associated with the SysPrep tool. In the space provided, briefly describe the function of each component.

_____

_____

**Step 3.**   What security privileges must you possess to be able to run the SysPrep tool? What license requirements must you meet? Can you use the SysPrep tool to upgrade a computer?

_____

_____

**Step 4.**   Briefly describe the steps that occur when the SysPrep tool runs. Upon completion of system preparation, what tasks must be completed to set up the ThinkTech classroom?

_____

_____

# LAB ANALYSIS TEST

**1.** How can an administrator prevent the wrong RIPrep image from being installed on a client computer?

_____

_____

**2.** Should all computers that wish to install a RIPrep image have identical hardware?

_____

_____

**3.** When the user interaction level of the SysPrep Setup Manager is set to GUI Attended, what is the result?

_____

_____

**4.** Why must a DHCP server be configured and active on the network when clients are being allowed to connect a RIS server?

_____

_____

**5.** Is the initial (primary) computer security ID (SID) removed when the SysPrep program runs? Give reasons for your answer.

_____

_____

# KEY TERM QUIZ

Use the following vocabulary terms to complete the sentences below. Not all of the terms will be used.

Deploy.cab

group policy

pre-execution environment (PXE)

remote boot disk generator

remote installation preparation wizard (RIPrep)

Remote Installation Services (RIS)

system preparation (SysPrep)

unattend.ini

unattend.txt

1. The _____ tool is provided by Windows XP to remove machine-specific information from a computer so that it can be imaged in the future.

2. The _____ provides the ability to prepare an existing Windows XP Professional installation, including locally installed applications and specific configuration settings, for imaging and to replicate the image to a remote server on the network.

3. A(n) _____-compliant network card enables a computer to boot remotely over the network.

4. You can use _____ to control client installation options and to prevent the wrong image of Windows XP Professional from being installed on a client computer.

5. The _____ file is an answer file used to answer basic configuration questions in an unattended installation.

# LAB WRAP-UP

You should now be familiar with the process of implementing a scripted unattended Windows XP Professional installation. You should also understand the process of establishing a RIS server, and creating a RIPrep image for installation. Finally, you have examined Setup Manager and should now know how to use SysPrep to prepare a computer for imaging.

# LAB SOLUTIONS FOR CHAPTER 3

In this section, you'll find solutions to the lab exercises, lab analysis test, and key term quiz.

## Lab Solution 3.01

This solution outlines how you might plan the installation of several Windows XP Professional computers in a large company.

**Step 1.**   The tools required for creating an answer file for an unattended installation of Windows XP Professional are the Deploy.cab file and Setup Manager. The Deploy.cab file contains the Setup Manager, and Setup Manager is used to create the answer file.

**Step 2.**   The Deploy.cab file is located in the \Support\Tools folder on the Windows XP Professional CD.

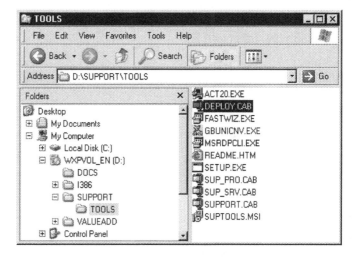

**Step 3.**   In Setup Manager, you should select the Create a New Answer File option. You should also indicate that the answer file is for a Windows Unattended Installation and that the Windows XP Professional platform is being installed.

**Step 4.**  To satisfy the requirement that you alone can view the pages of the installation as it progresses, you should choose the Read Only level of user interaction.

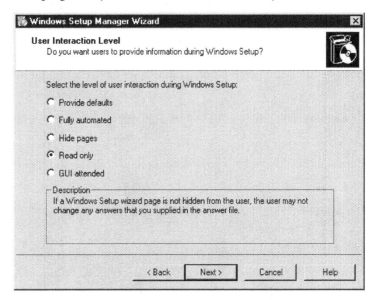

**Step 5.**  You should choose to create a new distribution folder and to copy the files from the CD. You need to specify the location and share name of the newly created distribution folder, as shown in Figure 3-1.

---

**FIGURE 3-1**

Specifying the location and share name of a new distribution folder

> **Windows Setup Manager Wizard**
>
> **Distribution Folder Name**
> You can create or modify a distribution folder.
>
> Would you like to create a new distribution folder or modify an existing one?
>
> ⦿ Create a new distribution folder
>
> ◯ Modify an existing distribution folder
>
> Distribution folder:
> `C:\Distribution`                          Browse...
>
> Share as:
> `Distribution`
>
> < Back    Next >    Cancel    Help

FIGURE 3-2 Customizing the software

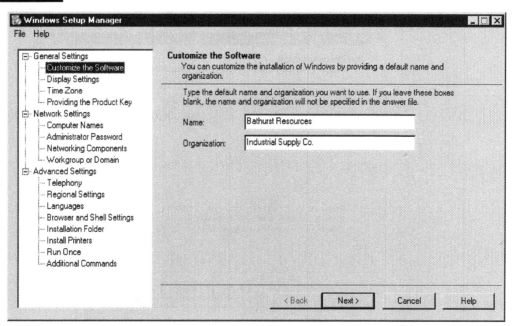

**Step 6.** Figure 3-2 shows one of the various settings for the Bathurst Resources answer file. Though not all of the settings are illustrated here, all settings must be entered as specified in Step 6 of the scenario as shown in Table 3-1.

**Step 7.** The UNC path should show the location and name of the answer file:

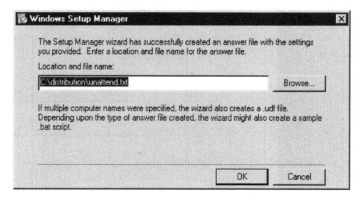

| TABLE 3-1 | | |
|---|---|---|
| | **Name** | Bathurst Resources |
| Use this information to customize the answer file settings for Bathurst Resources | **Organization** | Industrial Supply Co. |
| | **Colors** | True color (32 bit) |
| | **Screen area** | 800×600 |
| | **Refresh frequency** | Use Windows default |
| | **Time zone** | (GMT -04:00) Atlantic Time (Canada) |
| | **Product key** | Enter the Product Key from your personal CD |
| | **Computer names** | TestComputer |
| | **Administrator password** | 200%@BRC (choose to have the password encrypted) |
| | **Networking components** | Typical settings |
| | **Windows Server domain** | Domain1 (Computer account: Administrator; Password: password) |

**Step 8.**   Once the answer file exists, you can use the Winnt32.exe program to begin the unattended installation of Windows XP Professional. The syntax for running the unattended setup is

```
Winnt32 /s: c:\Distribution /u:c:\Distribution\unattend.txt
```

where:

- **/s: c:\Distribution**   specifies the location of the Windows XP Professional installation files—in this case, the shared Distribution folder.

- **/u:c:\Distribution\unattend.txt**   specifies that the installation is unattended and that the answer file, unattend.txt, is located in the Distribution folder on the C: drive.

## Lab Solution 3.02

Creating your RIS installation image should have involved the tasks outlined here.

**Step 1.**   At the London location, a Windows 2000 RIS server has to be configured in an Active Directory domain. DNS and DHCP must be active in the domain, and clients from the Edinburgh and Glasgow locations must be able to connect to the Windows 2000 server. The DHCP server must also authenticate the RIS server.

At the Edinburgh or Glasgow location, you must create a RIPrep image. If the client computers at either location lack pre-execution environment (PXE)–enabled network adapter cards, then RIS boot disks must be created at each location, and the PCI network adapters on the client computers must be supported.

**Step 2.**  You can use the Windows Components wizard to install RIS:

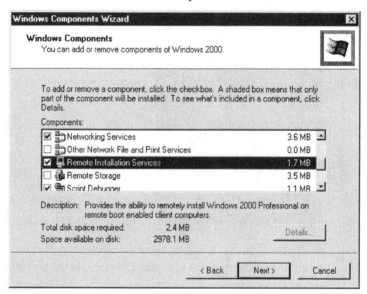

Be sure to configure the initial client settings as shown here:

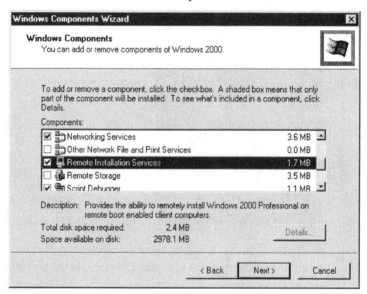

**Step 3.**   To authorize the RIS server, complete these steps:

1. Log on to the Windows 2000 DHCP server.

2. Click Start | Programs | Administrative Tools | DHCP.

3. In the DHCP window, right-click DHCP, and click Add Server. In the dialog box that opens, type the IP address of the RIS Server, and click OK.

4. Right-click DHCP and click Manage Authorized Servers.

5. Select the RIS server and click Authorize. Click OK.

You must have domain administrator rights to authorize a RIS Server in the Active Directory domain.

**Step 4.**   The Remote Boot Disk Generator window should indicate the selected floppy drive:

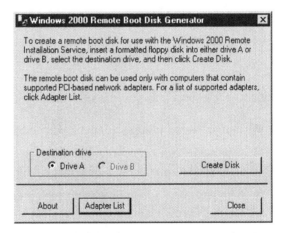

**Step 5.**   To create the RIPrep image, complete these steps:

1. At the Windows XP Professional computer, connect to the Windows 2000 RIS server, and run the RIPrep.exe program. You can find RIPrep.exe in \\ *servername*\\*RISsharename*\Admin\I386\RIPrep.exe.

2. The Welcome screen for the Remote Installation Preparation wizard opens. Click Next.

3. The wizard prompts you for the name of the Windows 2000 RIS server to which the image is to be copied. Click Next.

4. Choose the RemoteInstall folder to which the image is to be copied. Click Next.

5. The Friendly Description and Help Text window opens. Click Next.

6. Review the summary. Click Next. The image is copied to the Windows 2000 RIS server.

# Lab Solution 3.03

Planning your work before attempting to carry it out is always a good idea. Here is what you should consider when planning to use SysPrep for unattended installations of Windows XP Professional.

**Step 1.**  To use the System Preparation tool, install Windows XP Professional on the desired computer, configure the operating system, apply any service packs, and install any desired applications. SysPrep images are designed to be used on computers that have the same hardware as the machine on which the image was created. You should therefore ensure that all student computers in the ThinkTech classroom have identical hardware. The only exceptions are minor Plug and Play devices (sound cards, modems, etc.).

**Step 2.**  The four components associated with system preparation are these:

■  SysPrep.exe, the application that generates the image.

■  SysPrep.inf, an answer file that automates the mini-setup portion so that that the installation process is completely hands-free.

■  Setyupcl.exe, a program that runs the mini-setup wizard and generates unique security IDs for both the source and destination computers.

■  Mini-setup wizard, a wizard that asks users some final questions, such as agreement of the End User License Agreement (EULA) and the product key, domain, and username (among others).

**Step 3.**  You must be an administrator on the Windows XP computer to run SysPrep, and you must have a volume licensing agreement with Microsoft to comply with the EULA. SysPrep is used for clean installations only; you cannot upgrade a computer using a SysPrep image.

**Step 4.** Once you have prepared the source computer by installing the Windows XP Professional operating system, all services packs, and all desired applications, you can run the SysPrep tool. SysPrep removes the security ID from the source computer. Once the preparation is complete, SysPrep reboots the computer. After startup, the Mini-setup wizard appears, and the computer receives a new security ID. Finally, to capture an image for distribution to the classroom student computers, you must run a third-party imaging software package.

## ANSWERS TO LAB ANALYSIS TEST

1. Using group policies and NTFS permissions, you can control client installation options and prevent the wrong image from being installed on a client computer.

2. To be able to accept a RIPrep image, all client computers need not have identical hardware. They must all have the same hardware abstraction layer, but Plug and Play will handle other hardware differences in the systems.

3. When the user interaction level of the SysPrep Setup Manager is set to GUI Attended, only the text-mode portion of Windows setup is automated.

4. RIS clients cannot access a RIS server without an IP address lease from the DHCP server. A DHCP server must therefore be configured and active on the network when clients are attempting to connect.

5. To ensure that an image does not contain a security ID, SysPrep removes the security ID of the source computer before creating the image.

## ANSWERS TO KEY TERM QUIZ

1. system preparation (SysPrep)

2. remote installation preparation wizard (RIPrep)

3. pre-execution environment

4. group policy

5. unattend.txt

# 4

# Configuring and Troubleshooting the Desktop Environment

## LAB EXERCISES

Managing a user's desktop settings is a common task for a network administrator. Many companies require that their users maintain identical desktop settings. Certain users may require accessibility options; other users may prefer customized desktop settings. Windows XP Professional provides tools and settings that can accommodate users and administrators for configuring and troubleshooting the desktop environment.

This chapter examines the various desktop settings that are configurable with Windows XP Professional. You will configure accessibility features, implement desktop policies, examine regional and language options, and configure user profiles.

## LAB EXERCISE 4.01

# Examining Accessibility Options

**30 Minutes**

Rolf owns a small software development company. He has several users that require the accessibility options available with the Windows XP Professional operating system. The table that follows lists the users and their various needs.

| User | Accessibility need |
| --- | --- |
| Pamela – mobility impairment | Repeated keystrokes must be ignored |
| Liz – hearing impairment | Programs that generate sounds must provide text captions |
| Aaron – vision impairment | Text displayed on monitor must be enlarged |
| Dimitri – mobility impairment | Keyboard must be mouse-driven |

## Learning Objectives

In this lab, you examine the various accessibility options available on a Windows XP Professional computer. At the end of the lab, you'll be able to

- Identify keyboard options for mobility-impaired users.
- Identify sound options for hearing-impaired users.
- Identify display options for visually impaired users.

## Lab Materials and Setup

The materials you need for this lab are

- Pencil and paper
- Computer with Windows XP Professional installed

## Getting Down to Business

Accessibility for users with various physical impairments is a crucial aspect of computing today. In this lab, you look at some of the ways that Windows XP Professional accommodates users with special needs.

**Step 1.** In the space provided, list the methods that are available with Windows XP Professional for deploying accessibility options.

_____

_____

**Step 2.** At the Control Panel, double-click the accessibility options icon. Looking at the Keyboard tab, which options would suit Pamela's needs?

_____

_____

**Step 3.** At the Control Panel, double-click the accessibility options icon. Looking at the Sounds tab, which options would suit Liz's needs?

_____

_____

**Step 4.** Choose Programs | Accessories |Accessibility, and open the accessibility tool that would suit Aaron's needs. What is the name and function of the tool?

_____

_____

**Step 5.** Choose Programs | Accessories |Accessibility, and open the on-screen keyboard. Looking at the on-screen keyboard, what three typing modes are available for typing data? How will the on-screen keyboard help Dimitri?

_____

_____

**Step 6.** What other accessibility utility is available for visually impaired users? Briefly describe the function of that utility in the space provided.

_____

_____

**LAB EXERCISE 4.02**

# Configuring a Local Computer Policy to Manage Desktop Settings

**30 Minutes**

Keith provides technical support to Café Constantine, a local Internet coffee shop. Cathy, the owner of the coffee shop, has asked Keith to ensure that the Windows XP Professional computer available to her customers always maintains a compulsory desktop setting. In the past, Cathy has had problems with users adding shortcuts and files to the desktop. She wants to prevent such additions from happening in the future. She wants the desktop on the computer to display a JPEG image that advertises Café Constantine. She would also like to prevent users from changing any Active Desktop content.

## Learning Objectives

In this lab, you configure a local computer policy to manage the desktop settings for all users that sit at a particular Windows XP Professional computer. After you've completed the lab, you'll be able to

- Configure mandatory wallpaper settings.
- Configure Active Desktop settings.

## Lab Materials and Setup

The materials you need for this lab are

■ Pencil and paper
■ Windows XP Professional computer

## Getting Down to Business

These steps guide you in using the Group Policy administrative tool to create a local computer policy for Café Constantine.

**Step 1.** At the Windows XP Professional computer, run the Microsoft Management Console from the Start menu.

**Step 2.** From the File menu of the Microsoft Management Console, select Add/Remove Snap-in.

**Step 3.** In the Add/Remove Snap-in window, choose to add a snap-in. In the Add Standalone Snap-in window that opens, choose to add a Group Policy.

**Step 4.** In the Select Group Policy Object window that opens, verify that Local Computer appears in the Group Policy Object field. Close the window, saving the change. Close the Add Standalone Snap-in window.

**Step 5.** Verify that the Local Computer policy item appears in the Add/Remove Snap-in window. Close the window.

**Step 6.** At the Microsoft Management Console, expand the Local Computer Policy object. Expand the User Configuration object. Expand the Administrative Templates object. Expand the Desktop object. Select the Active Desktop object.

**Step 7.** Enable the Active Desktop object.

**Step 8.** To preventing users at Café Constantine from making changes to the desktop of the Windows XP Professional computer, enable the Prohibit Changes object.

**Step 9.**   Indicate the path to the location of the Active Desktop wallpaper that Cathy wishes to use on the computer at Café Constantine. (Note that, before a path to the wallpaper can be entered in the field, the wallpaper has to be enabled.)

**Step 10.**   Expand the Control Panel object, and select the Display object.

**Step 11.**   Enable Remove Display in the Control Panel object. This step removes the Display object from the Control Panel, preventing Café customers from using that object to make changes.

**Step 12.**   To create a local Group Policy, what permissions are necessary on the local computer? Can you configure a policy on a per-user basis?

_____

_____

## LAB EXERCISE 4.03

# Examining Regional and Language Options    **30 Minutes**

Brian has recently moved from New York to London, England. His Windows XP Professional computer is still showing regional options from the United States. He now wants to the change how currencies are displayed on his computer. He also wants to install support for the English (United Kingdom) language option.

## Learning Objectives

In this lab, you configure the regional and language options so that they suit Brian's needs in England. At then end of the lab, you'll be able to

- Configure regional currency formats.
- Configure language options.

## Lab Materials and Setup

For this lab exercise, you'll need

- Pencil and paper
- Computer with Windows XP Professional installed

## Getting Down to Business

In Windows XP Professional, you can set a number of options that adapt the computer for work in a particular country. In the steps that follow, you'll practice setting those options.

**Step 1.** At the Control Panel, double-click the regional and language options icon.

**Step 2.** At the Regional and Language Options window, select English (United Kingdom). Note that the samples have been updated to reflect the English (United Kingdom) format. Select the Customize button to check for other changes.

**Step 3.** At the Customize Regional Options window, select the Currency tab. Note that the currency options have been modified to include the British pound currency symbol. Save the new currency format.

**Step 4.** Select the Languages tab. Click Details, and then click Add to reach the Add Input Language window. Select English (United Kingdom).

**Step 5.** Select Key Settings. At the Advanced Key Settings window, make sure that Brian can easily switch input languages. Choose Ctrl+Shift for making the switch.

## LAB EXERCISE 4.04

# Creating and Managing Local User Profiles     **30 Minutes**

Cheryl has asked that her user account have the same desktop settings as Mike's user account. Both Cheryl and Mike have local user accounts on the same Windows XP Professional computer. You decide to copy Mike's user profile to Cheryl's local user account.

## Learning Objectives

In this lab, you create a local user profile and copy it to another local user account. At the end of the lab, you'll be able to

- Create a local user account.
- Configure a local user profile.
- Copy a local user profile.

## Lab Materials and Setup

For this lab exercise, you'll need

- Pencil and paper
- Computer with Windows XP Professional installed

## Getting Down to Business

**Step 1.**  Log on to the Windows XP Professional computer using the local administrator account.

lab
**Hint**

*The local administrator account is the administrator account that is stored on the local computer and that can be viewed from the Computer Management | Local Users and Groups tool. A domain administrator account is stored on a domain controller. To log on to a domain administrator account, you must choose a domain in the Logon dialog box.*

Right-click the My Computer object, and select Manage. Expand Local Users and Groups, and choose to add a new user.

**Step 2.**  Create a new user (called Mike) with a blank password. Configure the account so that the user is not required to change the password at the next logon.

Create a new user (called Cheryl) with a blank password. Configure the account so that the user is not required to change the password at the next logon.

Close the New User dialog box, and close the Computer Management window.

**Step 3.** Log off the Windows XP Professional computer. Log back on as Mike. Open the desktop Properties dialog. Apply the Windows Classic theme to the computer. Log off the computer.

Log on to the computer as Cheryl. Log off the computer.

lab
**(i)int** *Logging onto the computer and altering the desktop settings creates a unique user profile for Mike's user account. Logging onto the computer as Cheryl ensures that a profile is created for Cheryl's account.*

lab
**Warning** *Be sure to log each user off; do not use the Switch User option.*

**Step 4.** Log on to the computer using the local administrator account. Open the Properties dialog for My Computer. On the Advanced tab, go to the settings for User Profiles.

**Step 5.** Select Mike's profile from the list of user profiles, and copy it to the folder where Cheryl's profile is stored.

**Step 6.** When prompted, confirm the copy operation. Close all open windows. Log off the computer.

**Step 7.** Log on to the local computer as Cheryl. Verify that the Windows Classic theme has been applied to Cheryl's account.

# LAB ANALYSIS TEST

1. The Switch User option of Windows XP Professional allows more than one user to be logged on locally at a particular computer. Is it possible to copy one user's profile to another user's profile if both users are currently logged on? Briefly give reasons for your answer.

   _____

   _____

2. When you are creating a Local Computer policy, what does the Not Configured setting for an object imply?

   _____

   _____

3. When you are making use of more than one language on Windows XP Professional, how can you easily switch from one language to the other?

   _____

   _____

4. What is the difference between a local user profile and a roaming user profile?

   _____

   _____

5. What is the purpose of the ToggleKeys accessibility feature?

   _____

   _____

# KEY TERM QUIZ

Use the following vocabulary terms to complete the sentences below. Not all of the terms will be used.

Accessibility wizard

accessibility options

BounceKeys

FilterKeys

group policy

magnifier

mandatory profile

narrator

on-screen keyboard

regional options

roaming user profile

StickyKeys

ToggleKeys

Utility Manager

Windows Installer packages

1. Using _____ users can check an accessibility program's status and start or stop an accessibility program.

2. _____ are single-file packages that contain all of the necessary components (such as .exe and .dll files) to install an application.

3. _____ is a keyboard feature that instructs the system to ignore brief or repeated keystrokes.

4. A(n) _____ is a server-based user profile that is downloaded to the local computer when a user logs on and that is updated both locally and on the server when the user logs off.

5. _____ enables "simultaneous" keystrokes even though the keys are pressed one at a time.

## LAB WRAP-UP

You have now examined the various desktop settings that are configurable with Windows XP Professional. You should be familiar with the many accessibility features and how to configure those features. You have also learned how to implement desktop policies, how to examine regional and language options, and how to configure user profiles.

# LAB SOLUTIONS FOR CHAPTER 4

In this section, you'll find solutions to the lab exercises, lab analysis test, and key term quiz.

## Lab Solution 4.01

To accommodate the special needs of the users in the scenario, you should have used an approach similar to that described in the steps that follow.

**Step 1.**    Accessibility options can be deployed either through the Accessibility icon in the Control Panel, or through the Accessibility wizard, which you can start from the Programs | Accessories | Accessibility menu. The Utility Manager, also found in the Accessibility menu, can also be used to deploy tools such as the narrator, magnifier, and on-screen keyboard.

**Step 2.**    The Keyboard tab in the Accessibility Properties dialog shows the Use FilterKeys keyboard option selected:

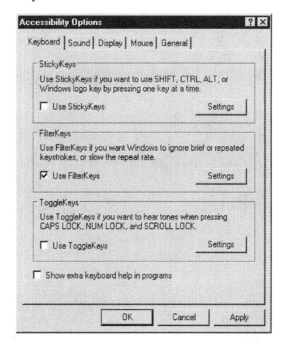

If you click Settings, the Filter Options should be set for the FilterKeys to Ignore Repeated Keystrokes.

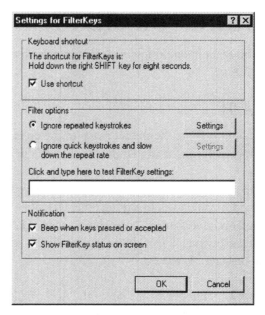

Those options will meet Pamela's needs.

**Step 3.** For Liz to see text captions for the sounds that are made by programs on her computer, the ShowSounds option should be selected:

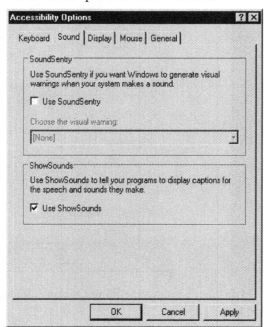

**Step 4.**   The Microsoft magnifier introduction message should be shown:

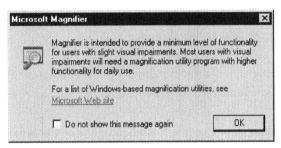

The magnifier is a display utility that makes the screen more readable for users who have impaired vision. The magnifier creates a separate window that shows a magnified portion of the screen.

**Step 5.**   Figure 4-1 shows the on-screen keyboard.

The on-screen keyboard is a utility that displays a virtual keyboard on the screen. The on-screen keyboard has three typing modes:

- In *clicking mode,* you click the on-screen keys to type text.
- In *scanning mode,* the on-screen keyboard continually scans the keyboard and highlights areas where you can type keyboard characters by pressing a hot key or using a switch-input device.
- In *hovering mode,* you use a mouse or joystick to point to a key for a predefined period of time; the selected character is then typed automatically.

In hovering mode, Dimitri will be able to type data using a mouse.

**Step 6.**   The narrator is a text-to-speech utility for users who are blind or have impaired vision. The narrator reads what is displayed on the screen: the contents of the active window, menu options, or typed text.

**FIGURE 4-1**

Viewing the
on-screen keyboard

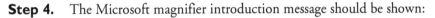

## Lab Solution 4.02

Your solution for Cathy at Café Constantine should resemble the solution presented in the next group of steps.

**Step 1.**   At the Windows XP Professional computer, select Start and then Run. Type **mmc** into the space provided, and click OK.

**Step 2.**   The Microsoft Management Console opens (Figure 4-2). From the File menu of the console, select Add/Remove snap-in.

**Step 3.**   When you begin, the Add/Remove Snap-in window is empty (Figure 4-3). Select Add. The Add Standalone Snap-in window that opens shows the list of snap-in tools available.
   Scroll to and select Group Policy from the list of snap-ins. Click Add (Figure 4-4).

**Step 4.**   In the Group Policy wizard, make sure that the Group Policy Object is stored on the Local Computer. Click Finish. In the Add Standalone Snap-in window, click Close.

**FIGURE 4-2**   Adding a snap-in to the Microsoft Management Console

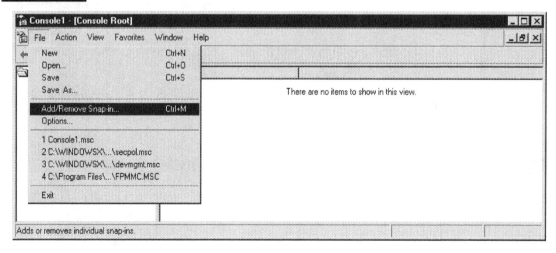

FIGURE 4-3

Opening the
Add/Remove
Snap-in dialog
in preparation
for adding a
snap-in

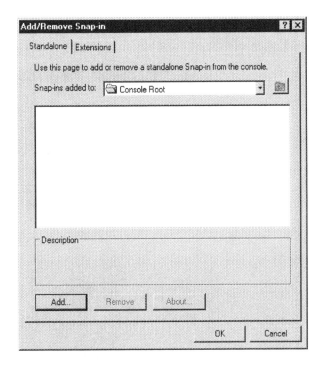

FIGURE 4-4

Choosing a
Group Policy
snap-in to add

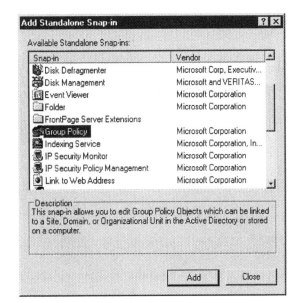

**Step 5.** The Local Computer Policy that now appears in the list of snap-in tools will appear in the Microsoft Management Console.

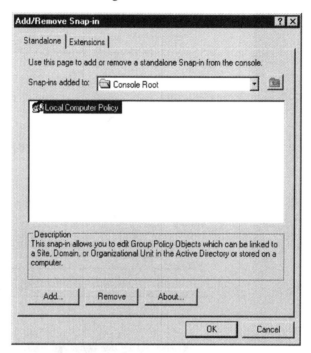

Click OK to close the window.

**Step 6.** Figure 4-5 shows the Active Desktop object in the Local Computer policy for user configuration.

**Step 7.** Enable the Active Desktop: Double-click the Active Desktop object, select the Enabled radio button (Figure 4-6), and click OK.

**Step 8.** To prevent changes to the desktop of the Windows XP Professional computer, double-click the Prohibit Changes object. Select the Enabled radio button (Figure 4-7). Click OK.

**Step 9.** To indicate the path to the location of the Active Desktop wallpaper, double-click the Active Desktop Wallpaper object, and select the Enabled radio button (Figure 4-8). Into the Wallpaper Name field, enter this path:

```
c:\windows\web\wallpaper\cafe.jpg
```

Click OK.

**FIGURE 4-5**  Viewing the new Active Desktop object in the Local Computer policy for user configuration

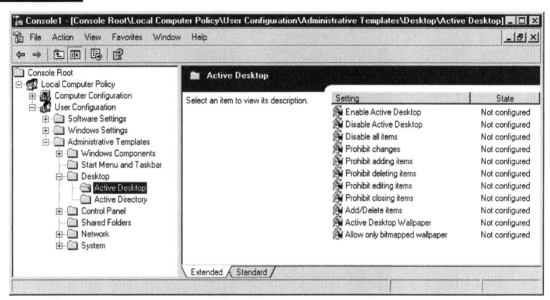

**FIGURE 4-6**

Choosing
to enable
Active Desktop

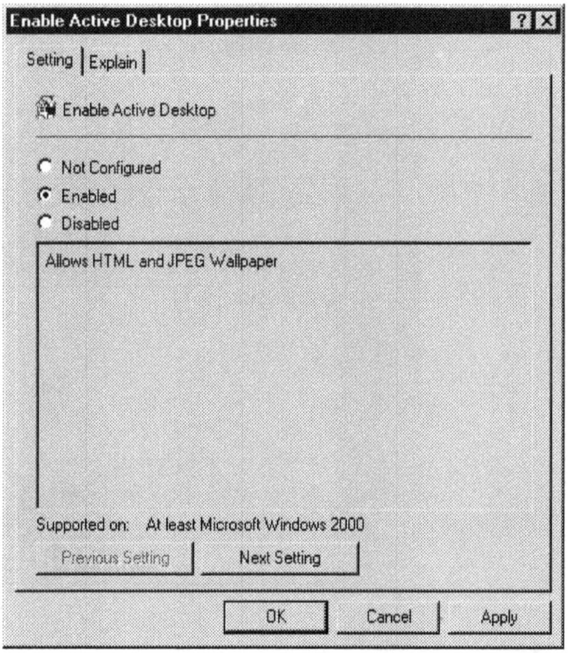

**FIGURE 4-7**

Enabling
the Prohibit
Changes option
so that users
cannot change
the desktop

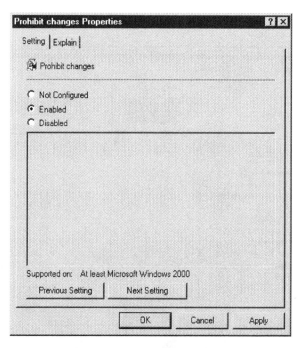

**FIGURE 4-8**

Choosing
and enabling
a wallpaper
for the desktop

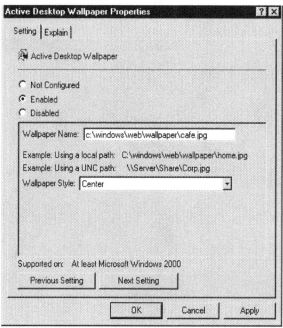

**FIGURE 4-9**   Confirming the Display object in the Microsoft Management Console

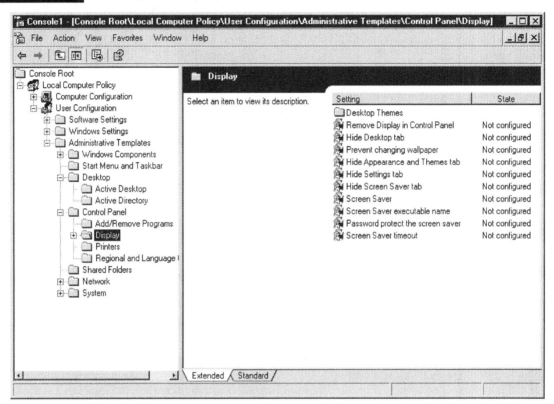

**Step 10.**   In the left windowpane, expand the Control Panel object. Select the Display object. Figure 4-9 shows the Display object in the Microsoft Management Console.

**Step 11.**   Double-click Remove Display in the Control Panel object, and select the Enabled radio button (Figure 4-10). Click OK.

**Step 12.**   You must be an administrator on the local Windows XP Professional computer to create a Local Group Policy. The Group Policy that you create affects all users who log on to the computer; you cannot single out users and individually apply the Local Group Policy to one of them.

**FIGURE 4-10**

Removing the
Display icon from
the computer's
Control Panel

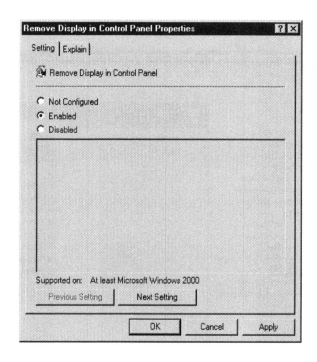

## Lab Solution 4.03

Your solution for Brian's regional and language set-up needs should resemble the
solution described here.

**Step 1.** Figure 4-11 shows the Regional and Language Options object that
you can use to configure the currency and language options. You will find
English (United Kingdom) on the Standards and Formats drop-down list.

**FIGURE 4-11**

Finding the Regional
and Language
Options object

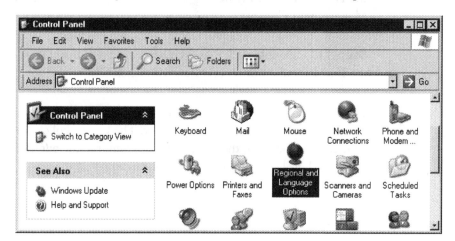

**Step 2.** The Regional Options window shows the desired United Kingdom format for language:

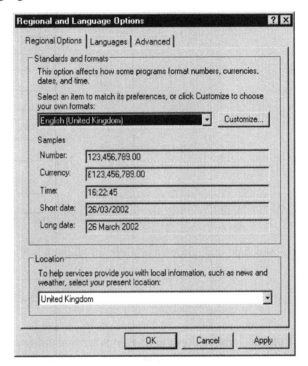

The United Kingdom location has also been selected. That option helps other services to provide the user with local information.

**Step 3.** The Currency tab of the Regional Options dialog shows the correct currency format for the United Kingdom (Figure 4-12). Click OK to save the new currency format.

**Step 4.** The Add Input Language window is used to choose the English (United Kingdom) language option from the Input Language drop-down list (Figure 4-13).

The English (United Kingdom) language option should be added to the list of installed Text Services (Figure 4-14).

**FIGURE 4-12**

Checking the currency symbol setting in the Regional Options dialog

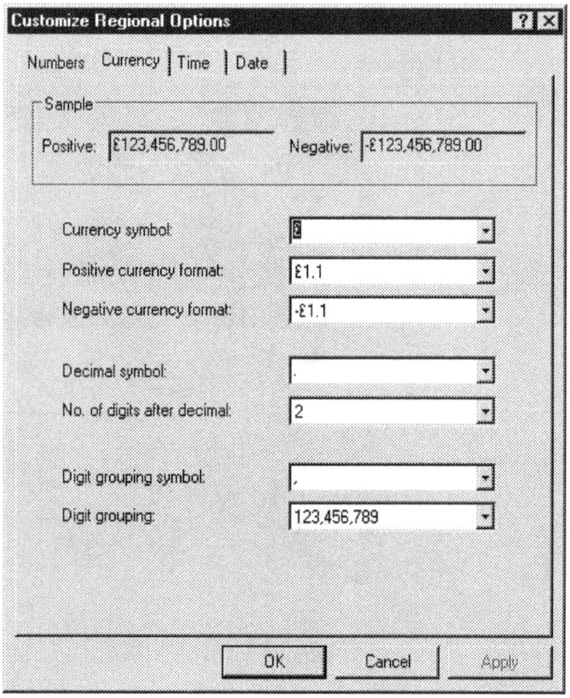

**Step 5.** At the Advanced Key Settings window, select Change Key Sequence. Ensure that the Switch Input Languages check box is selected. Select the Ctrl+Shift radio button. Click OK to close the Change Key Sequence window. The Advanced Key Settings window now shows that the Ctrl+Shift key sequence is to be used to switch between input languages (Figure 4-15)

Click OK to close the Advanced Key Settings window.

**FIGURE 4-13**

Adding English (United Kingdom) as an input language

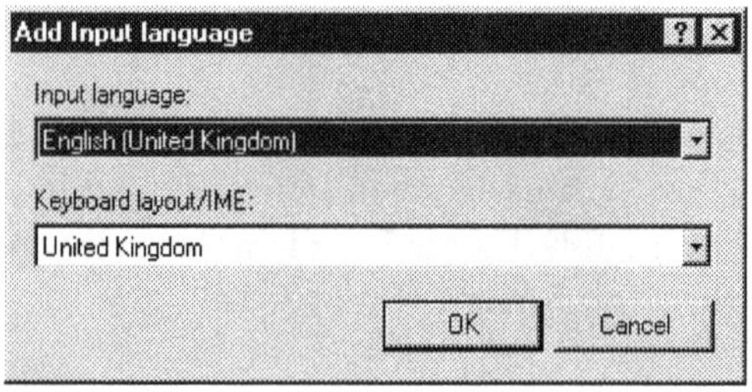

**FIGURE 4-14**

Checking that the
installed Text
Services now
include English
(United Kingdom)

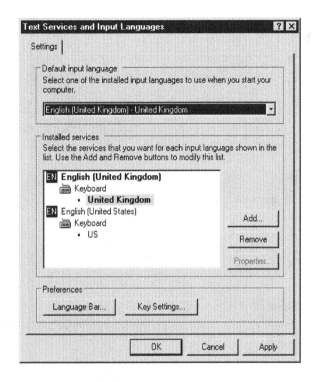

**FIGURE 4-15**

Confirming
that Ctrl+Shift
is now used to
switch between
input languages

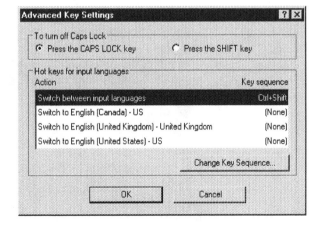

## Lab Solution 4.04

When you set Cheryl's account to use the same desktop settings as Mike's account, your approach should have been similar to one described here.

**Step 1.**   From the Computer Management tool, select Local Users and Groups, and then select the Users folder. Right-click Users, and click New User in the context menu. The new user will be created in the Users folder.

**Step 2.**   The process of creating the Mike and Cheryl accounts includes specifying the username for each account. Optional items include configuring a full name and a description for the user. In this exercise, choose simply to create the username. To prevent the situation in which the user must change the password at the next logon, clear the check box labeled User Must Change Password At Next Logon, and then click Create.

**Step 3.**   Right-click the desktop and choose Properties. The Display Properties window opens. Choose the Windows Classic theme from the Display Settings dialog (Figure 4-16). Click OK.

Choosing the Windows Classic theme in the properties dialog for the display screen

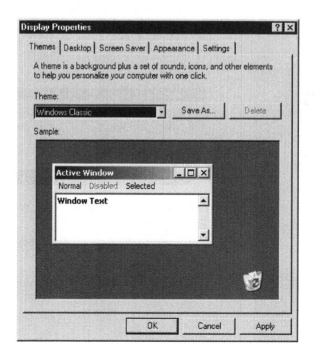

**Step 4.** Right-click My Computer, and select Properties. Click the Advanced tab. Click the Settings button for User Profiles.

Here is an example of User Profiles that have been created on a local computer:

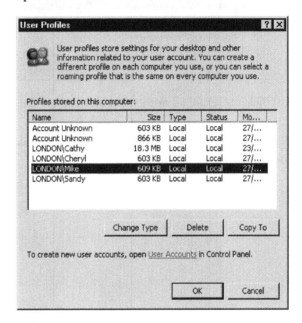

**Step 5.** In the list of user profiles, right-click Mike's profile, and select Copy To. In the Copy To dialog box, click Browse. Browse to the C:\Documents and Settings\Cheryl folder, and click OK. The path to Cheryl's profile folder, to which the Mike account profile will be copied, should look like this:

**Step 6.** A message asks you to confirm that you want to copy new information to the existing Cheryl profile:

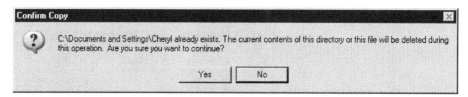

Click Yes. Close all open windows. Log off the computer.

**Step 7.** When you log on as Cheryl, the Windows Classic theme should appear for the account.

# ANSWERS TO LAB ANALYSIS TEST

1. If, during an attempt to copy one user's profile to another user account, both users are currently logged on, the copy fails. For example, if the Switch User option was used instead of the Log Off option, the user accounts are still logged on, and one user's profile cannot be copied to another user account.

2. The Not Configured option means that policy is not invoked. No registry settings are made concerning a Not Configured policy object. On the other hand, the Enable and Disable settings do write information to the registry. If all of the settings are enabled or disabled, Windows XP Professional requires more time to boot because the registry has to process all of the settings. If you are applying multiple policies using the same objects, a setting of Enabled or Disabled from a second applied policy can override the Not Configured option setting for the object.

3. Go to the Languages tab of Regional and Language Options Properties dialog. On the Languages tab, click Details. Once you have configured the second language, you can click Language Bar and place an icon in the Notification area or configure a toggle key to switch back and forth.

4. A local user profile is stored on the local computer. It is used when users log on to that particular computer. A roaming user profile is typically stored on a server (as in a domain environment). Roaming profiles are beneficial to users who work at several different computers each day, but who want the same documents and settings regardless of where they log on.

5. ToggleKeys are an accessibility feature. ToggleKeys sets the keyboard to beep when one of the locking keys (CAPS LOCK, NUM LOCK, or SCROLL LOCK) is switched on or off. The setting is helpful if you find yourself accidentally pressing CAPS LOCK, NUM LOCK, or SCROLL LOCK from time to time. The tones let you know that one of the keys has been pressed.

# ANSWERS TO KEY TERM QUIZ

1. Utility Manager

2. Windows Installer packages

3. FilterKeys

4. roaming user profile

5. StickyKeys

MICROSOFT CERTIFIED SYSTEMS ENGINEER

# 5

# Managing Windows XP Hardware

## LAB EXERCISES

W indows XP Professional is not only a fully compliant Plug and Play system, it also provides many tools for installing and managing computer hardware. This chapter examines the Add Hardware wizard, the File Signature Verification utility, and the Device Manager utility. All of these Windows XP Professional tools help in managing computer hardware. In the labs in this chapter, you will create a hardware profile, configure power options, examine driver signing, and examine display settings.

**LAB EXERCISE 5.01**

# Installing Hardware on Windows XP Professional

**30 Minutes**

Curtis has installed a new modem in his computer, but when he powers the computer on, the Windows XP Professional operating system fails to recognize the modem. Curtis has asked for your help in troubleshooting the problem.

## Learning Objectives

In this lab, you install hardware on a Windows XP Professional computer. At the end of the lab, you'll be able to

- Troubleshoot a failed hardware installation.
- Use the Add Hardware wizard to install a new modem.
- Verify the installation of the new hardware.

## Lab Materials and Setup

The materials you need for this lab are

- Pencil and paper
- Computer with Windows XP Professional installed

## Getting Down to Business

The steps that follow lead you through the process of installing a standard 56,000 bps modem through the Windows XP interface. You need not manually install the modem hardware, because this lab is strictly for demonstration purposes. If you already have a modem installed on your computer, you can still install a standard 56,000 bps modem without error.

**Step 1.**  At the Windows XP Professional computer, prepare to start the Add Hardware wizard. (You can start the wizard from the Hardware tab of the System Properties dialog or from the Control Panel.)

**Step 2.**  Start the Add Hardware Wizard, and click past the opening splash screen.

**lab**
**Hint**        *The Add Hardware wizard searches for uninstalled hardware.*

**Step 3.**  Indicate that you have already connected the hardware.

**Step 4.**  Choose to add a new hardware device.

**Step 5.**  Rather than having Windows XP Professional search for the hardware, choose to install a hardware device selected from a list.

**Step 6.**  The list of available devices should appear. Make sure that the Modems device category is selected.

**Step 7.**  Choose not to have Windows XP Professional detect the modem.

**Step 8.**  Select the standard 56,000 bps modem.

**Step 9.**  Select an available port from the list of ports provided.

**lab**
**Hint**        *Windows attempts to install the modem that you select.*

**Step 10.** You should successfully reach the completion stage of the Add Hardware wizard. Close the wizard and open the Device Manager.

**Step 11.** At the Device Manager, expand the Modems object and verify that the standard 56,000 bps modem is listed. Verify that the device is working properly. Uninstall the modem.

## LAB EXERCISE 5.02

# Creating a Hardware Profile

**30 Minutes**

Marco travels with his laptop computer. He also uses his laptop computer at the office when he is not traveling, and therefore needs the network card only on certain occasions. He wants the network card on his computer to be disabled when he has no need for it. He has asked you to configure his computer to accommodate his pattern of use.

## Learning Objectives

In this lab, you create a hardware profile for a computer running Windows XP Professional. At the end of the lab, you'll be able to

- Copy a hardware profile.
- Use the Device Manager.
- Configure a hardware profile.

## Lab Materials and Setup

The materials you need for this lab are

- Computer with Windows XP Professional operating system installed
- Network adapter installed in the Windows XP computer

## Getting Down to Business

To appropriately set up Marco's computer, use the procedure outlined here.

**Step 1.**   Starting from My Computer on the desktop, open the Hardware Profiles dialog.

**Step 2.**   The Hardware Profiles dialog shows a default profile: (Current). Create a new profile based on the default profile, and give it the name **Laptop Profile**. Verify that the Hardware Profiles window now contains two profiles, the default (Current) profile and Laptop Profile.

**Step 3.**   Restart the Windows XP Professional computer. Select the new hardware profile and log on to the computer.

**Step 4.**   Open the Device Manager. At the Device Manager dialog, expand the Network Adapters object.

**Step 5.**   Choose the available network adapter. At the General tab of the network adapter device, in the Device Usage drop-down menu, disable the network adapter.

**Step 6.**   Run a scan for hardware changes. Afterwards, select the network adapter. In Device Manager, the network adapter should now appear marked with a red X.

**Step 7.**   Reboot the Windows XP Professional computer, and select Laptop Profile. You should discover that the network adapter remains disabled.

## LAB EXERCISE 5.03

# Examining Driver Signing

**20 Minutes**

Ali has hired you as a consultant for her small news media company, Ditto News. She is concerned about the fact that Ditto News employees regularly need to download software from the Internet. She wants to ensure that no unsigned driver software is installed. She has asked for your help in that matter.

## Learning Objectives

In this lab, you examine the feature of driver signing on Windows XP Professional. At the end of the lab, you'll be able to

- Recognize the driver signing options on Windows XP Professional.
- Recommend a driver signing solution for a small company.
- Implement driver signing.
- Implement the File Signature Verification utility.

## Lab Materials and Setup

For this lab exercise, you'll need

- Pencil and paper
- Computer with Windows XP Professional installed
- Internet connection

## Getting Down to Business

To implement driver signing for the employees at Ditto News, use the steps given here.

**Step 1.**   Where can you access the driver signing options for Windows XP Professional? In the space provided, list and briefly describe each of the options.

_____

_____

**Step 2.**   To satisfy Ali's request, which driver signing option should be implemented on employee computers for Ditto News?

_____

_____

**Step 3.**   On your Windows XP Professional computer, configure the driver signing option to Block (never install unsigned driver software).

From the Driver Signing dialog, open the Help and Support Center window. Read the article titled "Designed for Microsoft Windows XP Logo." In the space provided, briefly list the possible side effects if you install device drivers that have not been digitally signed by Microsoft.

_____

_____

**Step 4.** Which utility can check existing files on computers used by Ditto News employees to make certain that the files are digitally signed? Where can you find that utility?

_____

_____

**LAB EXERCISE 5.04**

# Configuring Power Options

**20 Minutes**

Lauren works as a content producer for a political consulting firm. She often has days when she sits at her desktop computer for an hour and is then away from it for several minutes or hours. She wants to reduce the power consumption by some of her computer devices when she is away from the computer, but she wants to ensure that she does not have to manually reboot the computer when she returns to it. Lauren has asked for your recommendations on how she should configure her computer to meet her needs.

## Learning Objectives

In this lab, you configure power options on a Windows XP Professional computer. At the end of the lab, you'll be able to

- Examine power options.
- Configure a power scheme.
- Configure power-saving settings.

## Lab Materials and Setup

For this lab exercise, you'll need a computer with Windows XP Professional installed.

## Getting Down to Business

Here's how you can help Lauren conserve power.

**Step 1.** At the Control Panel, open Power Options dialog, and go to the Power Schemes tab.

**Step 2.** Configure the power scheme as shown here:

| Home/office desk scheme | Time |
|---|---|
| Turn off monitor | 10 minutes |
| Turn off hard disks | 45 minutes |

**Step 3.** Enable Advanced Power Management support.

**lab Warning** *Your computer must report that it can support this feature for it to be available to be enabled.*

**Step 4.** On the UPS tab, set American Power Conversion and Smart-UPS.

**lab Hint** *Because you may not have an uninterruptible power supply (UPS) attached to your computer, you won't configure that device in this lab.*

**LAB EXERCISE 5.05**

# Examining Display Settings

**30 Minutes**

Steven is considering upgrading his video card to a higher quality model. He also wants to learn more about the display settings available on his computer. He asks you to show him the various display settings that can be configured through Windows XP Professional.

Examining Display Settings **83**

## Learning Objectives

In this lab, you troubleshoot problem display settings on a Windows XP Professional computer. At the end of the lab, you'll be able to

- Identify color and display settings.
- Identify video adapter mode types.
- Define screen refresh rates.

## Lab Materials and Setup

For this lab exercise, you'll need

- Pencil and paper
- Computer with Windows XP Professional installed

## Getting Down to Business

To help Steven get his new video card working, use this procedure:

**Step 1.**   Right-click an empty area of the desktop, and click Properties. Click the Settings tab. From the Color Quality drop-down menu, adjust the color quality to the highest settings supported by your computer's video card. What does the value of the color quality settings represent?

_____

_____

**Step 2.**   On the Settings tab, click Advanced. Ensure that Dots Per Inch (DPI) is set to the default Normal Size (96 DPI). What does the Dots Per Inch value represent?

_____

_____

**Step 3.**   On the Adapter tab, click Properties to access the Device Manager Properties dialog for the video card. Click List All Modes. What type of information is found in the list of valid modes?

_____

_____

**Step 4.**   Select the Monitor tab. At the Screen Refresh drop-down list, examine the selected screen refresh rate. What does the value for the screen refresh rate represent?

_____

_____

**Step 5.**   Select the Troubleshoot tab. Examine the Write Combining check box option. What does Write Combining do in terms of performance for the display settings on a computer monitor?

_____

_____

**Step 6.**   Select the Color Management tab. What is the purpose of the Color Management tab?

_____

_____

# LAB ANALYSIS TEST

1.  Is there an advantage to using the Hardware wizard rather than the Device Manager when troubleshooting a problem device?

    _____

    _____

2.  Are Windows XP Professional drivers automatically signed?

    _____

    _____

3.  Does hibernation work on all Windows XP Professional computers?

    _____

    _____

4.  Can a user directly control whether a computer is ACPI compliant?

    _____

    _____

5.  What steps can be taken to troubleshoot a monitor that exhibits distortion?

    _____

    _____

# KEY TERM QUIZ

Use the following vocabulary terms to complete the sentences below. Not all of the terms will be used.

Add Hardware wizard

Advanced Power Management

Advanced Configuration Power Interface (ACPI)

Compact Disk File System (CDFS)

Device Manager

driver signing

Dots Per Inch (DPI)

Peripheral Component Interconnect (PCI)

sigverif utility

refresh rate

Universal Disk Format (UDF)

1. The frequency with which the video screen is retraced to prevent the image from flickering is knows as the _____ .

2. Using the _____ , you can identify unsigned system files and device driver files on your computer.

3. _____ is an open industry specification that defines power management on a wide range of mobile, desktop, and server computers and peripherals.

4. _____ is a specification introduced by Intel Corporation that defines a local bus system that allows up to 10 compliant expansion cards to be installed in the computer.

5. The _____ enables you to add new hardware or to troubleshoot hardware-related problems.

# LAB WRAP-UP

Whether you're an old hand at adding and managing hardware, or new to the tools you've examined in this chapter, you should now be familiar with how to add hardware to a computer running Windows XP Professional. As well, you should be familiar with the tools that Windows XP Professional provides for managing the hardware that you install.

# LAB SOLUTIONS FOR CHAPTER 5

In this section, you'll find solutions to the lab exercises, lab analysis test, and key term quiz.

## Lab Solution 5.01

To install a standard 56,000 bps modem through the Windows XP interface, you should have completed the steps as described below.

**Step 1.** Right-click My Computer and select Properties. The System Properties window opens. Select the Hardware tab, where you can find a button to start the Add Hardware wizard (Figure 5-1). (The wizard can also be started at the Control Panel.)

**Step 2.** Click Add Hardware Wizard. The Add Hardware wizard opens. Click Next to move past the splash screen.

**Step 3.** At the next screen, select Yes, I Have Already Connected The Hardware. Click Next.

**FIGURE 5-1**

Finding the
Add Hardware
Wizard button
in the System
properties dialog

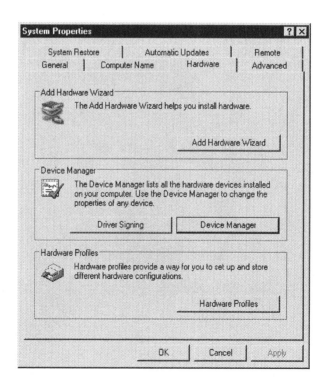

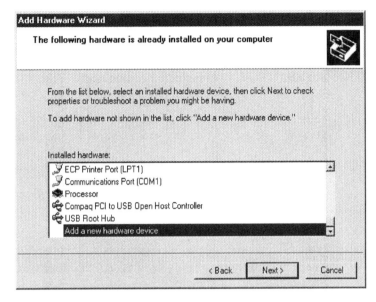

**FIGURE 5-2**

Choosing to add
a new hardware
device to a
Windows XP
Professional
computer

**Step 4.**   At the list of installed hardware, scroll to and select Add A New Hardware
Device (Figure 5-2). Click Next.

**Step 5.**   At the next screen, select Install The Hardware That I Manually Select
From A List (Advanced). Click Next.

**Step 6.**   From the list of available devices, select Modems (Figure 5-3). Click Next.

**FIGURE 5-3**

Choosing the
type of hardware
device to install

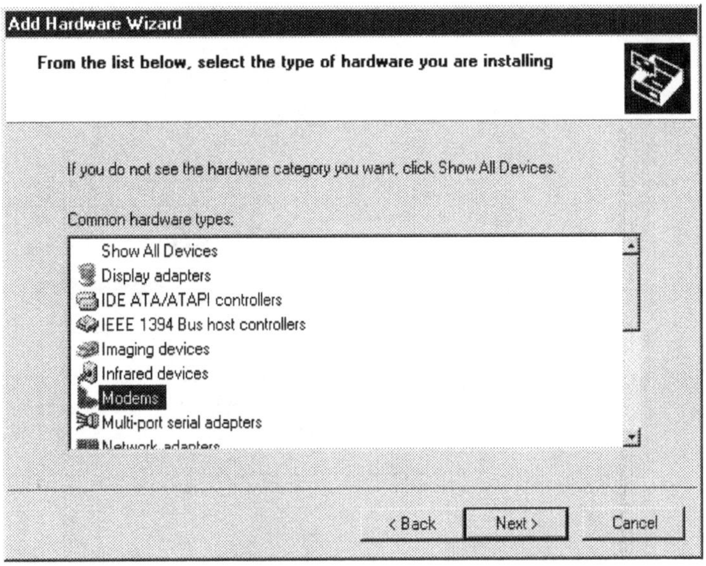

**Step 7.** At the next screen, select Don't Detect My Modem, I Will Select It From A List. Click Next.

**Step 8.** The list of standard modems available for installation should now open (Figure 5-4). From the list, select Standard 56,000 bps Modem. Click Next.

**Step 9.** At the next screen, you can select any available port. Click Next.

**Step 10.** Your modem should install successfully (Figure 5-5). Click Finish to close the wizard. At the Hardware tab of the System Properties dialog, click Device Manager. The Device Manager window opens.

**Step 11.** In the Device Manager dialog, double-click the Modems object to expand it. Verify that the standard 56,000 bps modem is listed (Figure 5-6).
  Double-click the modem. Check the Device Status on the General tab of the modem dialog (Figure 5-7).
  Right-click the modem and select Uninstall from the menu options.
  Close all open windows.

---

**FIGURE 5-4**

Choosing
the standard
56,000 bps
modem

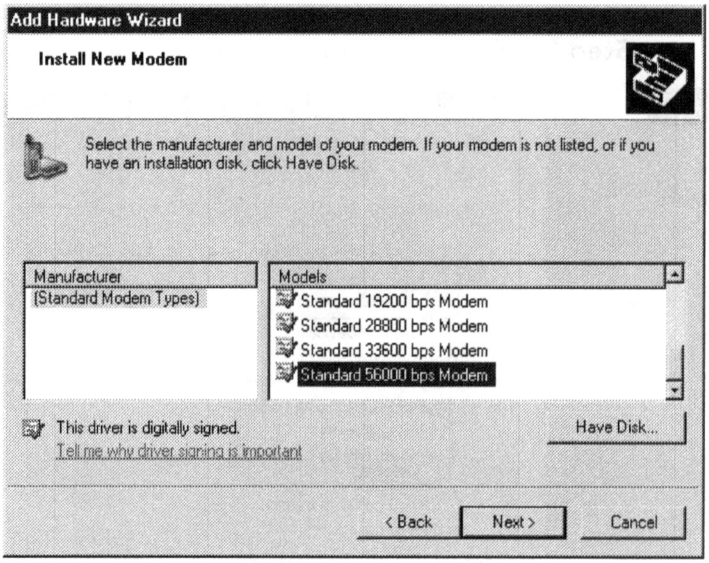

**FIGURE 5-5**

Reviewing
the successful
installation
of a modem

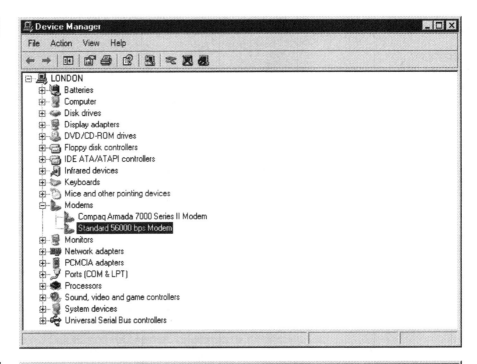

**FIGURE 5-6**

Verifying the
56,000 bps
modem in the
Device Manager

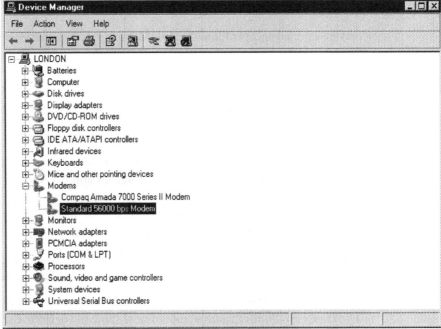

Checking the
status of a
hardware device
(modem)

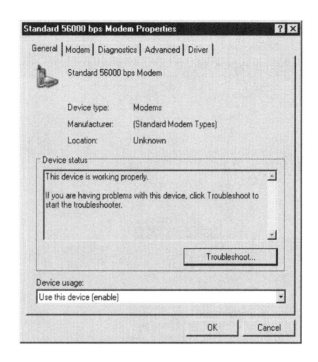

## Lab Solution 5.02

Setting up a second profile will allow Marco to easily disable the network card on
his computer when traveling.

**Step 1.** On the desktop, right-click My Computer, and select Properties. Select the
Hardware tab, and click the Hardware Profiles button. The Hardware Profiles window
opens (Figure 5-8).

**Step 2.** To create a new profile based on the default profile, click Copy. The
Copy Profile dialog box opens. Enter the name **Laptop Profile** in the To field:

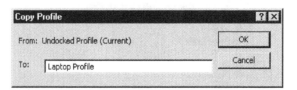

Click OK. The configuration of the default profile is copied to the new profile.
The Hardware Profiles window should now show the default (Current) profile and
the Laptop Profile (Figure 5-9).

**FIGURE 5-8**

Reviewing the
current list
of available
hardware profiles

Click OK to close the Hardware Profiles window. Click OK to close the System
Properties window.

**FIGURE 5-9**

Confirming that
a new profile has
been added to
the list of
available profiles

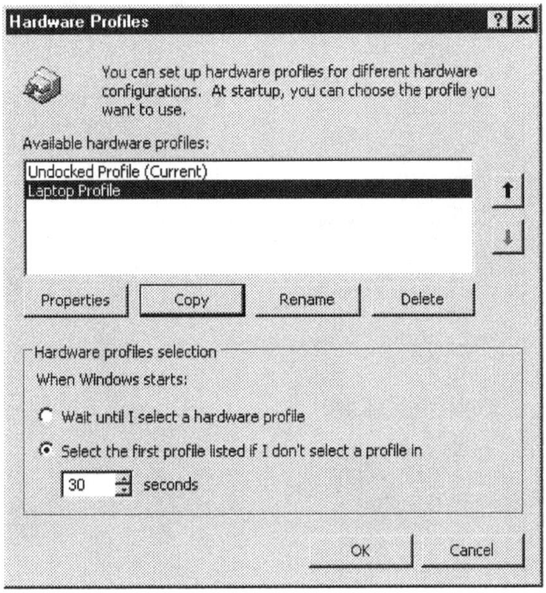

**Step 3.**   Restart the Windows XP Professional computer. Upon boot-up, a hardware profile menu appears. Select the newly created Laptop Profile and allow Windows XP to boot using that hardware profile. Log on to the computer.

**Step 4.**   From the desktop, right-click My Computer, and select Properties. Select the Hardware tab, and click the Device Manager button. At the Device Manager dialog, expand the Network Adapters object (Figure 5-10).

**Step 5.**   Double-click the available network adapter. In the device dialog that opens, choose the General tab. Open the Device Usage menu, and choose Do Not Use This Device In The Current Hardware Profile (Disable) option (Figure 5-11). Click OK.

**Step 6.**   Right-click the network adapter, and choose Scan For Hardware Changes from the menu (Figure 5-12).

When the scan is done, select the network adapter. Device Manager should show the network adapter as disabled (Figure 5-13).

**Step 7.**   Upon rebooting the computer and selecting the Laptop Profile, you should see that the network adapter is still marked as disabled in Device Manager.

| FIGURE 5-10 | |
|---|---|

Viewing the available network adapter devices in the Device Manager

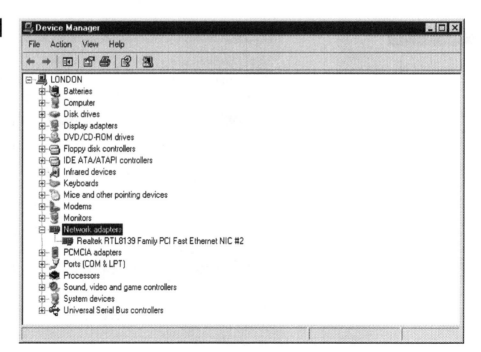

FIGURE 5-11

Choosing
to disable a
hardware device
(network adapter)

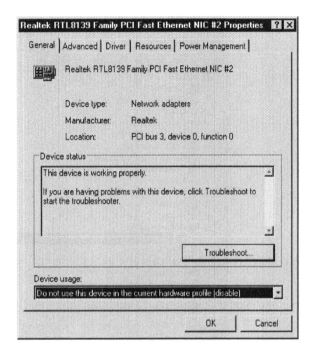

FIGURE 5-12

Choosing the
Scan For Hardware
Changes pop-up
menu option

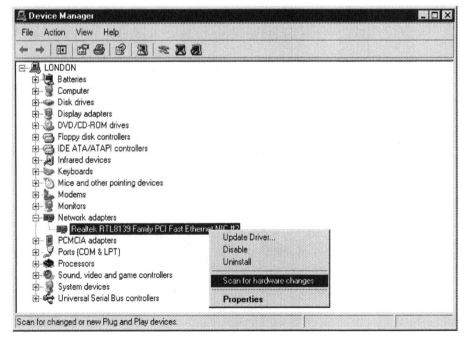

FIGURE 5-13

Viewing a disabled
hardware device
(network adapter)
in the Device
Manager

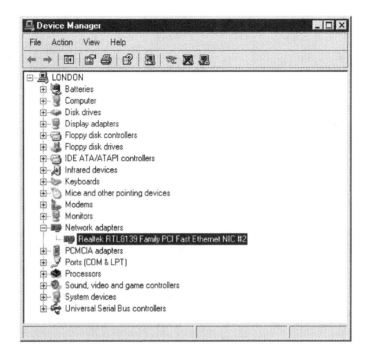

## Lab Solution 5.03

To help Ali make sure that no Ditto News employee downloads unsigned driver
software, you should have used a procedure resembling the one given here.

**Step 1.** The driver signing options are found in the System Properties at the
Hardware tab. These options can be invoked to determine how Windows XP
handles driver signing:

- **Ignore**   This option tells Windows to ignore the fact that software is not
  digitally signed and to install the software anyway. No warning messages or
  prompts are given when you use this setting.

- **Warn**   A warning dialog opens to alert you when a driver is not digitally
  signed. You can choose to install the driver. This setting is the default.

- **Block**   If a driver is not digitally signed, the operating system will not allow
  it to be installed.

- **Administrator option**   Selecting the Administrator check box makes the
  selected Ignore, Warn, or Block setting the default for all users on this particular
  Windows XP computer. You must be an administrator on the local computer to
  enable or disable this option.

**Step 2.**    Employee computers at Ditto News should implement the Block driver signing option. That option will prevent unsigned drivers from being installed.

**Step 3.**    Right-click My Computer, and select Properties. Select the Hardware tab. Click Driver Signing. Configure the driver signing option to Block. Click OK.

In the Driver Signing dialog, click Tell Me Why This Testing Is Important. The Help and Support Center window opens. Read the article "Designed for Microsoft Windows XP Logo."

Microsoft recommends you use only device drivers with the Designed for Microsoft Windows XP logo, because installing device drivers that have not been digitally signed may disable your system, allow viruses onto your computer, or otherwise impair the operation of your computer immediately or in the future.

**Step 4.**    The File Signature Verification utility can check existing files on Ditto News employee computers to make certain that they are digitally signed. To access the utility, run the sigverif command. You can also access the utility by choosing Programs | Accessories | System Tools | System Information. At the System Information window, select File Signature Verification from the Tools menu.

## Lab Solution 5.04

You should have configured Lauren's power settings as discussed in the steps that follow.

**Step 1.**    Click Start | Settings | Control Panel | Power Options. When the Power Options dialog opens, click the Power Schemes tab.

**Step 2.**    On the Power Schemes tab, select Home/Office Desk from the Power Schemes drop down menu. Configure the Home/Office Desk power scheme settings as indicated in the scenario:

| Home/office desk scheme | Time |
| --- | --- |
| Turn off monitor | 10 minutes |
| Turn off hard disks | 45 minutes |

**Step 3.**    Select the Advanced tab. Select the Advanced Power Management Support option.

**Step 4.**  Select the UPS tab, and click Select. In the UPS Selection dialog, select American Power Conversion from the Manufacturer drop-down menu. Select Smart-UPS from the model list. Click Finish. The UPS tab should now show the Smart-UPS model.

## Lab Solution 5.05

You should have described the various display settings to Steven in the ways discussed here.

**Step 1.**  Color quality settings value represents the number of colors that you would like your screen to display. Choose Medium to display more than 65,000 colors; High to display more than 16 million colors; and Highest to display more than 4 billion colors. Choosing more colors improves the color quality of the screen display, but a higher setting also means that more time is required to load screen display completely—for example, when opening a picture file in a web browser.

**Step 2.**  The Dots Per Inch standard is used to measure screen and printer resolution. The value is expressed as the number of dots that a device can display or print per linear inch. The greater the number of dots per inch, the better the resolution on the screen or on the printed page.

**Step 3.**  The list of valid modes shows all screen resolution modes that are supported by the video card installed on the computer. Each mode on the list comprises a screen resolution, color quality, and screen refresh rate.

**Step 4.**  Higher screen refresh rates reduce "flicker" that may appear on the screen. The higher quality of the video card that you install, the higher the possible refresh rate. The default refresh rate settings typically fall around 75 Hz – 85 Hz.

**Step 5.**  Write Combining provides graphics data to the monitor screen faster, improving performance. Some video cards cannot keep up with this setting. If you want to enable the Write Combining option, a high quality video card is typically required. If you are having distortion problems, clearing this check box may eliminate those problems.

**Step 6.** At the Color Management tab, you can choose a color profile that manages the display of colors on your monitor. Windows XP Professional provides a number of default profiles. If you choose a color profile specific to the monitor type, the color performance may improve. As a general rule, use a color profile only if you are having color-specific problems, because otherwise, a profile may limit your monitor's color capabilities.

## ANSWERS TO LAB ANALYSIS TEST

1. There is no advantage to using the Add Hardware wizard rather than the Device Manager to troubleshoot a problem device. The General tab for the device in the Device Manager tells you the device status and allows you to use the troubleshooter. The Add Hardware wizard provides the same capability.

2. Microsoft digitally signs all Windows XP Professional drivers. You can run the File Signature Verification utility sigverif to verify the signatures.

3. Windows XP Professional supports hibernation, but if hibernation is to work, it must also be supported by the computer's BIOS.

4. Users do not directly control ACPI compliance for a computer. During a Windows XP installation, the operating system detects ACPI compliance and invokes the standard.

5. If a monitor exhibits distortion, you can troubleshoot the problem by removing the Write Combining setting on the Troubleshoot tab of the Advanced Properties dialog. If making that change fails to solve the problem, you can reduce the hardware acceleration until the problem resolves.

## ANSWERS TO KEY TERM QUIZ

1. refresh rate

2. sigverif utility

3. Advanced Configuration Power Interface (ACPI)

4. Peripheral Component Interconnect (PCI)

5. Add Hardware wizard

MICROSOFT CERTIFIED SYSTEMS ENGINEER

# 6

# Configuring and Managing Windows XP Devices

## LAB EXERCISES

This chapter examines the process of configuring and managing devices with Windows XP Professional. Windows XP supports typical hardware and peripherals such as keyboards, pointing devices, modems, and printers. Additionally, Windows XP provides support for digital cameras, scanners, and wireless devices. The labs in this chapter will help you become familiar with installing, configuring, and managing such devices.

**LAB EXERCISE 6.01**

# Configuring a Keyboard and Mouse

**20 Minutes**

You aren't satisfied with the current responsiveness of your keyboard and mouse, and you want to change how those devices react when you use them. You decide to change the default keyboard configuration options. You also plan to configure your mouse with a new double-click speed and pointer display settings.

## Learning Objectives

In this lab, you configure keyboard and mouse options for a Windows XP Professional user. At the end of the lab, you'll be able to

- Configure keyboard character and cursor options.
- Configure mouse pointer options.

## Lab Materials and Setup

The materials you need for this lab are

- Pencil and paper
- Computer with Windows XP Professional installed
- Keyboard
- Mouse

## Getting Down to Business

In this lab, you have to apply the knowledge that you acquired in the *MCSE Windows XP Professional Study Guide* for configuring keyboard and mouse options.

**Step 1.** Record the original settings for the keyboard and mouse options shown in Table 6-1; then, configure each device as indicated in the New Setting column of the table.

**Step 2.** Briefly define the purpose of each setting that you configured for your keyboard and mouse in step 1.

_____

_____

**Step 3.** What are the functions of the Snap To and Visibility mouse options? In the space provided, briefly describe each one.

_____

_____

**Step 4.** Reverse the settings that you configured in step 1, returning to your original mouse and keyboard configuration.

| TABLE 6-1 | Option | Original setting | New setting |
|---|---|---|---|
| Keyboard and Mouse Configuration Settings | Repeat Delay | | Short |
| | Repeat Rate | | 50% Slow/fast |
| | Cursor Blink Rate | | Fast |
| | Double-Click Speed | | Slow |
| | Pointer Scheme | | Old Fashioned (system scheme) |
| | Enable Pointer Shadow | | Disabled |
| | Pointer Motion | | Fast |
| | Pointer Trails | | Display long pointer trails |

## LAB EXERCISE 6.02

# Configuring Phone and Modem Options

**30 Minutes**

Ann is in a hotel room in Calgary, Canada. She wants to configure the modem on her laptop computer to quietly dial the access number for an Internet service provider in Winnipeg, Canada. The hotel telephone requires that she dial 9 to access an outside line. Ann wants to ensure that her computer waits for a dial tone before attempting to make a call. She also wants the dialing rules to account for the different area codes for Calgary and Winnipeg when making the long-distance call. Ann knows that the area code for Calgary is 403.

## Learning Objectives

In this lab, you configure telephone and modem options that will satisfy Ann's needs. At the end of the lab, you'll be able to

- Configure dialing rules.
- Configure modem options.

## Lab Materials and Setup

The materials that you need for this lab are a computer with Windows XP Professional and a modem installed.

## Getting Down to Business

In this lab, you practice applying the knowledge you acquired about modems and dialing rules in the *MCSE Windows XP Professional Study Guide*.

**Step 1.** At the Control Panel on your Windows XP Professional computer, double-click Phone and Modems Options, and configure Calgary as a new location. Configure the dialing rules to satisfy Ann's needs as described.

**Step 2.** At the Modems tab, select your modem. Configure it to dial silently and to wait for a dial tone when making a connection.

**lab Hint** *If you do not have a modem (physical device) installed on your computer, a standard 56,000 bps modem should still appear in the list if you installed it in lab 5.01. If no modem appears in the list, you can follow the steps in lab 5.01 to install the standard 56,000 bps modem before you continue.*

**Step 3.** Select the Diagnostics tab in the Modem properties dialog. What is the purpose of the Query Modem button on that tab?

_____

_____

**Step 4.** Select the Advanced tab. What options can you set when changing the default preferences for the modem?

_____

_____

## LAB EXERCISE 6.03

# Troubleshooting a USB Device

**30 Minutes**

You are the administrator of your company's network. You have a functioning external universal serial bus (USB) hub, to which you would like to connect two USB devices. When connecting one of the USB devices to this USB hub, you discover that the device does not work.

## Learning Objectives

In this lab, you troubleshoot a USB device that is not working. At the end of the lab, you'll be able to

■ Identify the process of installing a USB device.

■ Identify the use of USB hubs.

■ Recommend a solution to solve a USB problem.

## Lab Materials and Setup

For this lab exercise, you'll need

- Pencil and paper
- Computer with Windows XP Professional installed

## Getting Down to Business

**Step 1.**  What is the standard process for installing a USB device on a computer running Windows XP Professional? What is the function of the USB root hub?

_____

_____

**Step 2.**  What is the purpose of installing external USB hubs?

_____

_____

**Step 3.**  At your Windows XP Professional computer, open the Device Manager and select the USB root hub from the available devices. View the Power tab from the USB Root Hub Properties dialog. What types of items are, or can be, listed in the Attached Devices list? Why is the hub information important?

_____

_____

**Step 4.**  What would you recommend as a solution to the USB device problem as stated earlier?

_____

_____

## LAB EXERCISE 6.04

# Examining Wireless Links

**30 Minutes**

Vince is considering using a wireless link to transfer images from his new digital camera to his Windows XP Professional computer. He has asked you to briefly describe to him the configuration options that Windows XP Professional provides for wireless links.

Vince wants Windows XP Professional to notify him when infrared activity occurs. He also wants to store the images from his digital camera in a particular folder that he specifies.

## Learning Objectives

In this lab, you examine the configuration options for wireless links on a Windows XP Professional computer. At the end of the lab, you'll be able to identify the Wireless Link configuration options.

## Lab Materials and Setup

For this lab exercise, you'll need

- Pencil and paper
- Computer with Windows XP Professional and a built-in fast infrared data association (IrDA) port *or* an external infrared device (digital camera) installed

## Getting Down to Business

In this lab, you apply the knowledge that you acquired in the *MCSE Windows XP Professional Study Guide* for configuring a wireless link.

**Step 1.** Log on to your Windows XP Professional computer as an administrator. At the Control Panel, open Wireless Link.

*If Wireless Link does not appear in the Control Panel, you may need to install an external infrared device. You can also use the Add Hardware wizard to install a wireless link. For information on how to install an external infrared device, refer to Chapter 6 of the MCSE Windows XP Professional Study Guide by Curt Simmons (McGraw-Hill/Osborne, 2002).*

**Step 2.**   Briefly describe how Vince can use the options on the Infrared tab to suit his needs. At the Infrared tab, configure those options.

_____

_____

**Step 3.**   At the Image Transfer tab, configure the options that would suit Vince's needs.

**Step 4.**   After you install an infrared device, where can that device be located for viewing? What can you view from the IrDA Settings tab for the infrared device?

_____

_____

# LAB ANALYSIS TEST

1. If, in trying to use the modem, a laptop computer exhibits unsteady behavior, what setting can be configured to solve the problem?

   _____

   _____

2. What is the name of process for connecting multiple USB devices together?

   _____

   _____

3. What must you do if the Wireless Link object does not appear in the Control Panel and you want to use a wireless device?

   _____

   _____

4. If configured, when would an icon for an infrared device appear in the Taskbar?

   _____

   _____

5. If you install a Plug and Play USB device on a computer, and if the system fails to detect it, even though you know for certain that the device has been detected on other computers, what could be the cause of the problem?

   _____

   _____

# KEY TERM QUIZ

Use the following vocabulary terms to complete the sentences below. Not all of the terms will be used.

area code rules

ClickLock

dialing rules

fast infrared data association (IrDA)

infrared printing

Infrared Image Transfer Protocol

infrared networking (IrNET)

repeat delay

repeat rate

serial infrared data association (IrDA SIR)

universal asynchronous receiver/transmitter (UART)

universal serial bus (USB)

1. _____ enables point-to-point communication between two computers.

2. The most common type of IrDA is _____ , which can provide data transfer speeds of up to 115.2 Kbps.

3. Using _____ , you can select text or drag a file without having to continuously hold the mouse button down.

4. The _____ adjusts how quickly characters repeat when you hold a key down.

5. How modem users access outside lines or long-distance numbers can be configured in the _____ of the Phone and Modem dialog.

# LAB WRAP-UP

You should now be familiar with installing, configuring, and managing modems, USB devices, and infrared devices. Additionally, you should now be able to configure mouse and keyboard settings to your desired preferences.

# LAB SOLUTIONS FOR CHAPTER 6

In this section, you'll find solutions to the lab exercises, lab analysis test, and key term quiz.

## Lab Solution 6.01

The various options for the keyboard and mouse mean that all users can customize the operation of the computer interface to suit their personal preferences.

**Step 1.** Figures 6-1 through 6-4 show the keyboard and mouse settings as you should have implemented them for the scenario.

**Step 2.** Repeat Delay adjusts the amount of time that elapses before characters repeat.

Repeat Rate adjusts how quickly characters repeat when you hold a key down.

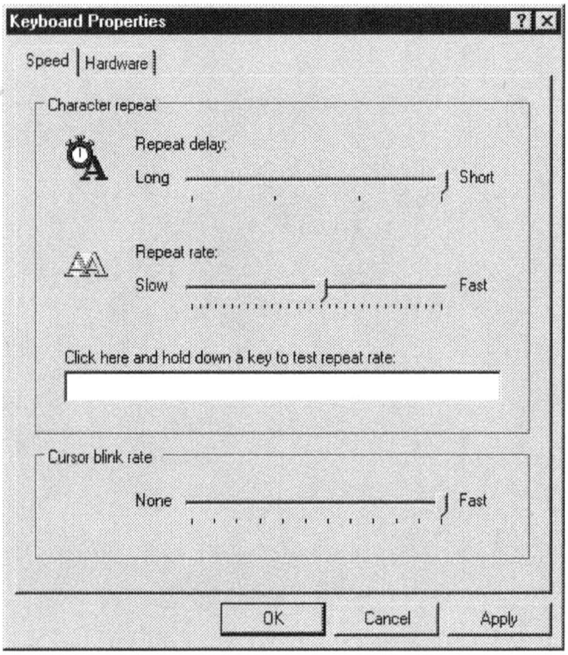

---

**FIGURE 6-1**

Setting the Keyboard Repeat delay, Repeat rate, and Cursor blink rate

**FIGURE 6-2**

Setting double-click
speed for a mouse
device

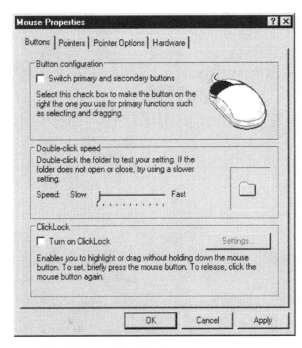

**FIGURE 6-3**

Choosing
a scheme for
the on-screen
pointer's
appearance

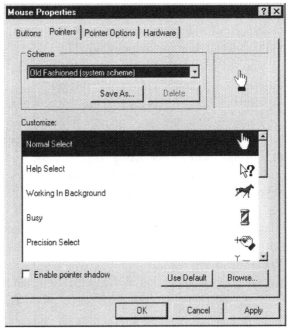

**FIGURE 6-4**

Setting various
options for the
on-screen pointer

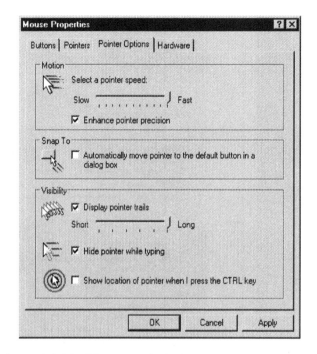

Cursor Blink Rate adjusts the rate at which the cursor blinks. To prevent the cursor (insertion point) from blinking, drag the slider to the left end of the bar. The cursor remains visible, but it will not blink.

Double-Click Speed adjusts the rate at which your mouse responds when you double-click the associated mouse button.

Pointer Scheme is any combination of pointers used on the desktop.

Enable Pointer Shadow displays a shadow under the pointer to give a 3-D effect.

Pointer Motion adjustments change how the pointer responds to the movements of the physical mouse device.

Pointer Trails displays a trail from the start position of the pointer to its destination as you use the mouse to move the pointer across the screen.

**Step 3.** The Snap To function automatically moves the pointer to the default button in a dialog box, reducing the need for you to make mouse movements. The Visibility options include pointer trails, which show where the pointer has been and the route to its destination. Additionally, you can hide the pointer while typing and show the location of the pointer by pressing the CTRL key.

**Step 4.** You should be able to easily reverse all changes that you made to the mouse and keyboard options.

## Lab Solution 6.02

Dialing options may require 10-digit numbers and special "line out" codes whether you are traveling or working in an office. Your solution for Ann should be similar to the one presented here.

**Step 1.**    Figure 6-5 shows dialing rules configured so that Ann can dial out from the 403 area code in Calgary, Alberta, Canada. The rules necessary for long distance and local calls are also shown.

Figure 6-6 shows how the new dialing rule is listed on the Dialing Rules tab.

**Step 2.**    Figure 6-7 shows the Modem tab configured with the speaker volume off ("silent dialing"), and the Dial Control set to wait for a dial tone before dialing the main number.

**FIGURE  6-5**

Configuring
the dialing rules
configured

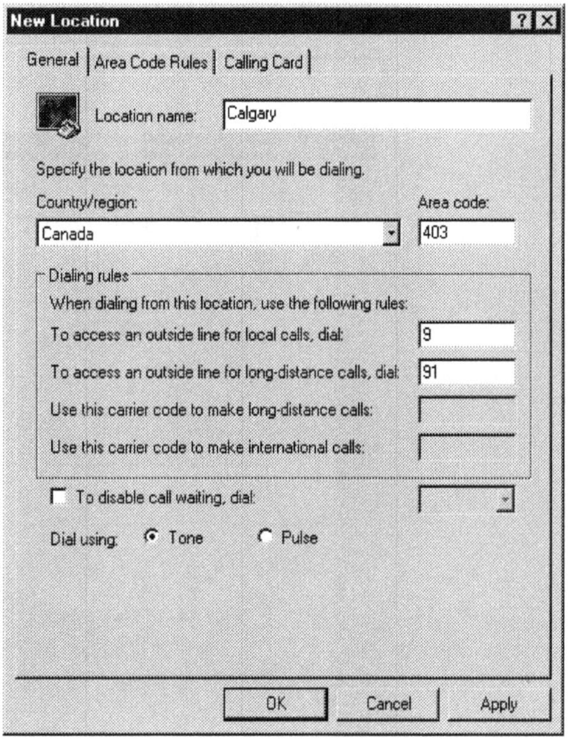

**FIGURE 6-6**

Checking the new rule on the Dialing Rules tab

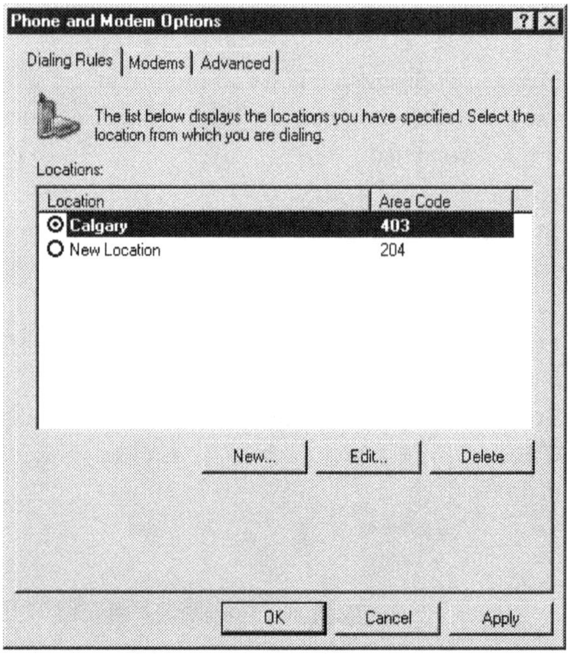

**FIGURE 6-7**

Choosing silent dialing and ensuring that a number is not dialed until a dial tone is heard

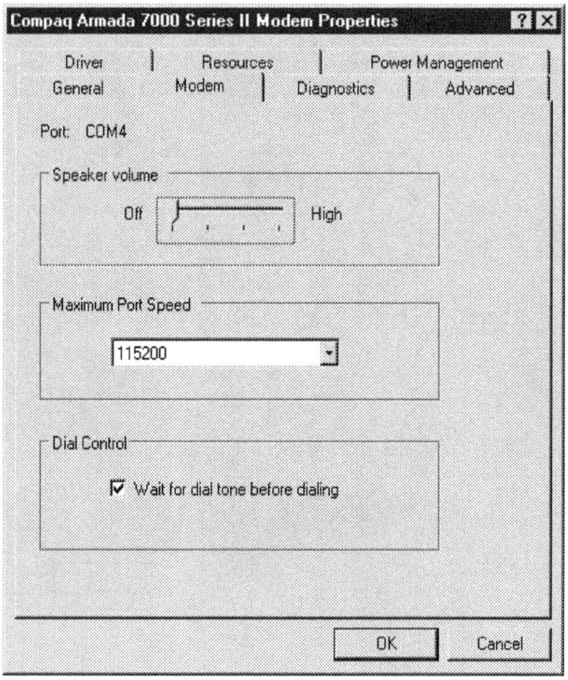

**FIGURE 6-8**

Locating the
Query Modem
button

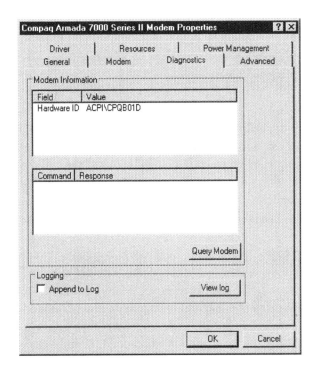

**Step 3.**    Figure 6-8 shows the Diagnostics tab of the modem properties dialog, where the Query Modem button is located. You can use the Query Modem button to verify that the modem is working properly. Windows XP Professional then issues a variety of commands to determine if the modem is functional. The results of the testing are then displayed.

**Step 4.**    If you click the Change Default Preferences button, you can see and set these options:

- Disconnect Call If Idle disconnects a call if the connection is idle for more than the defined number of minutes.
- Cancel Call If Not Connected disconnects a call if it fails to complete during the specified time. The call can be reinitiated if necessary.
- Port Speed determines how fast programs can transmit data to the modem.
- Data Protocol controls data error correction.
- Compression reduces the kilobyte size of data for transmission purposes.
- Flow Control specifies whether the flow of data between the modem and the computer is managed by the hardware or the software.

## Lab Solution 6.03

When a USB device fails to work, using the procedure described here should help you solve the problem.

**Step I.** When you install USB hardware, you simply plug the hardware into the USB port. Windows XP Professional automatically detects and installs the device with no interaction from you and no rebooting. The USB port found on the front or the back of a PC is called the USB root hub. The root hub connects directly to the motherboard. The USB root hub may have multiple USB ports available. In many cases, USB devices will also have their own ports so that you can daisy-chain a series of peripherals off one port.

**Step 2.** Using the USB root hub, you can connect several different USB devices, but you can also connect another external hub. USB hubs typically support up to seven additional connections, including another hub. The USB therefore has a *tiered star topology*. One hub feeds from the root hub, and the next hub feeds from the first hub, and so on. Using this tiered star topology, you can combine hubs to support up to 127 devices. Through additional USB hubs chained together, you can easily extend USB connections as you need them.

**Step 3.** The Attached Devices list may indicate the number of available ports, any USB devices, and any USB external ports. The hub information indicates how much power is available per port for any attached USB devices and the fact that the hub is self-powered.

**Step 4.** In the scenario, while connecting a USB device to the USB hub, you discovered that the device does not work. Chances are that the problem is related to power use. The external USB device that is not working needs more power to operate than the USB bus-powered hub can provide. To resolve the problem, you need a self-powered USB hub, which has its own connection to an independent power circuit.

## Lab Solution 6.04

To set up a wireless connection for Vince, you should have used a procedure resembling the one outlined here.

**Step I.** Find the Wireless Link icon in the Control Panel (Figure 6-9). Double-click the icon to open the associated dialog.

**FIGURE 6-9**

Finding the
Wireless Link
icon in the
Control Panel

**Step 2.** On the Infrared tab (Figure 6-10) of the Wireless Link dialog, Vince can choose the option Display An Icon On The Taskbar Indicating Infrared Activity to see icon on the Taskbar whenever infrared activity occurs.

**Step 3.** Figure 6-11 shows the Image transfer tab as it should be configured to accommodate Vince's needs.

**Step 4.** Figure 6-12 shows that the infrared device can be viewed from the Device Manager.

Figure 6-13 shows the IrDA Settings tab for the infrared device. Using the IrDA Settings tab, you can control the maximum connection rate for the IrDA device. The typical setting is 115,200 Kbps, but you can reduce that value if you are having problems transferring data from wireless devices.

**FIGURE 6-10**

Choosing to
show an icon
on the Taskbar
whenever infrared
activity occurs

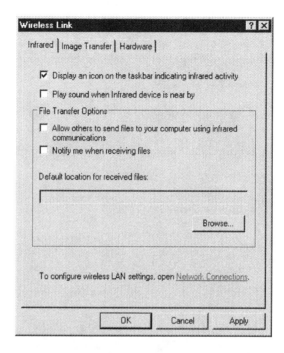

**FIGURE 6-11**

Setting Wireless
Link to transfer
images from a
digital camera
to a specific
folder on the
system

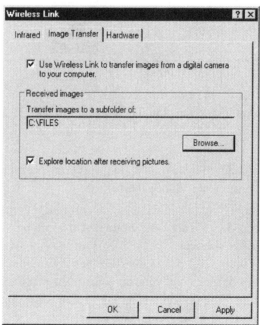

**FIGURE 6-12**

Checking the infrared device in Device Manager

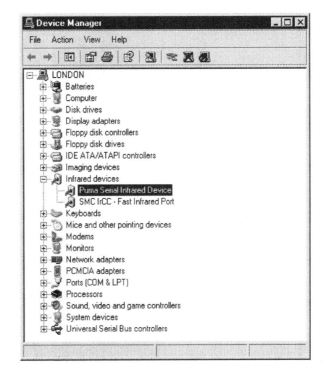

**FIGURE 6-13**

Controlling the connection rate for an infrared device

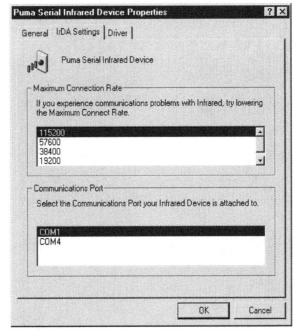

## ANSWERS TO LAB ANALYSIS TEST

1. Adjusting the port speed on the Modem tab of the modem's properties dialog will help to reduce the amount of information flowing from the modem to the computer at a given time and will solve the unsteadiness. The specified speed setting represents the maximum speed at which programs are allowed to transmit data to the modem. That speed is normally faster than the modem speed.

2. Connecting multiple USB devices to one another through USB ports is called daisy-chaining. For instance, a USB root hub may have multiple USB ports available. In many cases, USB devices even have their own ports, so that you can daisy-chain peripherals together off one port.

3. If the Wireless Link object does not appear in the Control Panel, you may need to install an external infrared device. Once you obtain the device, simply attach it to the appropriate serial or USB port, and installation will begin. You can also use the Add Hardware wizard to install a wireless link.

4. When an infrared device is in range of the port, an icon for the infrared device appears in the notification area. You can then choose to use the device and transfer files.

5. The problem may be that the BIOS of the computer that is not discovering the device is not configured for USB support. In that case, to enable USB you would have to request a new BIOS from the hardware manufacturer.

## ANSWERS TO KEY TERM QUIZ

1. infrared networking (IrNET)

2. serial infrared data association (IrDA SIR)

3. ClickLock

4. repeat rate

5. dialing rules

MICROSOFT CERTIFIED SYSTEMS ENGINEER

# 7

# Configuring Disk Drives and Volumes

**B**efore you begin working with data on a Windows XP Professional computer, it is always a good idea to establish the file system format, the management features that the hard disks are to support, and the limitations for data storage that are to be enforced. This chapter examines the NTFS file system that is supported by the Windows XP Professional operating system. In the labs, you will also troubleshoot a disk management problem and analyze the differences between basic and dynamic disks. Finally, you'll implement disk quotas on an NTFS-formatted drive to limit data storage by users.

**LAB EXERCISE 7.01**

# Examining the NTFS File System

**30 Minutes**

Connor wants to install the Windows XP Professional operating system on a computer he shares with his brother. Currently, he is familiar only with the Windows 98 operating system, which runs the FAT32 file system. He wants the files and folders that he creates in Windows XP Professional to be inaccessible to his brother. He asks you to explain to him the benefits of implementing NTFS on his computer and to recommend the appropriate file system for his needs.

## Learning Objectives

In this lab, you examine the features of the NTFS file system and recommend a file system solution for Connor's computer. At the end of the lab, you'll be able to

- Examine the features of the NTFS file system.
- Enable NTFS file security.
- Recommend a file system solution.

## Lab Materials and Setup

The materials you need for this lab are

- Pencil and paper
- Computer with Windows XP Professional installed
- NTFS-formatted disk drive

## Getting Down to Business

File system organization is central to the operation of any computer. Here's how you can answer Connor's questions about the file system for Windows XP Professional.

**Step 1.** In Windows Explorer on your XP Professional computer, create a folder called **Connor's Files** on the NTFS-formatted drive, and open the folder Properties.

---

---

**Step 2.** At the Properties tab, click the Advanced button. What feature among the Advanced Attributes would suit Connor's need for making the files in his folder inaccessible to his brother? Give reasons for your answer.

---

---

**Step 3.** Click Cancel at the Advanced Attributes dialog.

From the Tools menu in Windows Explorer, select Folder Options. Choose to disable simple file sharing.

*You will learn more about NTFS file sharing during the labs in Chapter 9. For now, disabling simple file sharing allows you to configure NTFS file security.*

**Step 4.** Open the Properties dialog for Connor's Files. A new tab has been added to the Properties dialog. What is its name? In the space provided, briefly describe the function of the new tab and its benefit to Connor's Files.

---

---

**Step 5.** Does the FAT32 file system provide any support for file security or encryption? Recommend a file-system solution for Connor's Windows XP Professional computer.

---

---

## LAB EXERCISE 7.02

# Troubleshooting Disk Management

**30 Minutes**

Lisa wants to create spanned volumes on her disk drive; but when she looks at the disk drive in the Disk Management console, she discovers that she has no option for creating spanned volumes. She asks you to troubleshoot and provide her with a solution to her problem. (Figure 7-1 shows Lisa's current disk configuration.)

## Learning Objectives

In this lab, you troubleshoot a disk management problem. At the end of the lab, you'll be able to

- Troubleshoot using the Disk Management tool.
- Define requirements for creating volumes.
- Define requirements for creating spanned volumes.

**FIGURE 7-1**   Reviewing Lisa's disk configuration

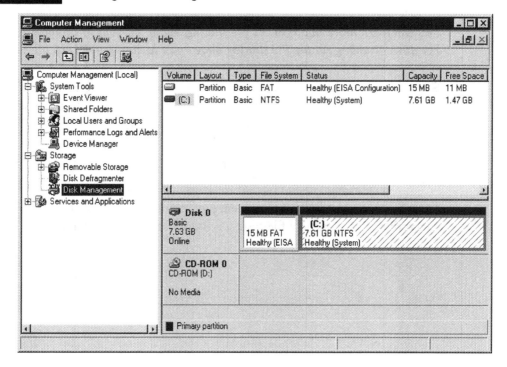

## Lab Materials and Setup

The materials you need for this lab are

- Pencil and paper
- Computer with Windows XP Professional installed

## Getting Down to Business

To help Lisa create spanned volumes, here's what to do.

**Step 1.** Based on the information contained in Figure 7-1, why is Lisa not able to view the option for creating a volume on her drive? What disk configuration changes must be made to provide support for creating volumes?

_____

_____

**Step 2.** What are the requirements for creating a spanned volume? List the steps that Lisa must complete to create a spanned volume on the Disk 0 drive.

_____

_____

**Step 3.** From the Administrative Tools menu on your Windows XP Professional computer, open the Computer Management console, and select Disk Management. View the current configuration of your Disk 0 hard drive. Note the properties of the disk in the space provided here.

_____

_____

**Step 4.** From your current Disk 0 configuration, what steps are required before you can create a spanned volume? What steps are necessary before you can create a simple volume? List your results in the space provided.

_____

_____

**LAB EXERCISE 7.03**

# Implementing Disk Quotas

**30 Minutes**

You have noticed that several users are storing large amounts of data on the NTFS-formatted drive, causing the drive to constantly run out of space. You want to limit data storage to a maximum of 200MB per user on the NTFS drive, and you want the system to warn users when they are approaching the maximum limit. A certain user named Mike has been storing many audio and video files on the computer. You want to prevent him from doing so in the future by limiting his storage space to 100MB.

## Learning Objectives

In this lab, you implement a disk quota for a user named Mike on the NTFS-formatted drive of your Windows XP Professional computer. At the end of the lab, you'll be able to

- Enable quota management.
- Create a quota entry for a particular user.
- Test a quota limit.

## Lab Materials and Setup

For this lab exercise, you'll need

- Pencil and paper
- Computer with Windows XP Professional installed
- NTFS-formatted disk drive
- Access to 100MB of data

## Getting Down to Business

In this lab, you apply the knowledge that you acquired in the *MCSE Windows XP Professional Study Guide* for implementing disk quotas.

**Step 1.** Log on to the Windows XP Professional computer as Administrator. At the Computer Management | Local Users and Groups | Users container, verify that the Mike account exists.

*If an account called Mike does not appear, you can use the Computer Management | Local Users and Groups console to create the user.*

Close any open windows. Open My Computer, and then open the Properties dialog for the NTFS-formatted drive. Go to the Quota tab.

**Step 2.** Choose to deny disk space to users exceeding the quota limit, and limit the disk space to 200MB. Choose to warn users when their data storage reaches 150MB.

**Step 3.** Create a new quota entry for Mike.

**Step 4.** Limit Mike's storage space to 100MB. Issue a warning to Mike when his data storage reaches 80MB. Apply all settings, and log off.

*You should receive a message warning that the volume will be rescanned to apply the new quota limits. Read the details of the warning, and click OK.*

**Step 5.** Log on as Mike. Browse to the NTFS-formatted drive. Right-click the drive to view its properties. On the General tab, check the free disk space and note the number in the space provided. Does the reported free space indicate that the quota limit is functioning properly?

_____

_____

**Step 6.** Try to copy 110MB of data to the NTFS-formatted drive on your computer. Note the results in the space provided.

_____

_____

## LAB ANALYSIS TEST

1. What are the primary features of the NTFS file system?

   _____

   _____

2. What are the states that a dynamic disk may display? List and define each state.

   _____

   _____

3. How can you extend a simple volume on a dynamic disk?

   _____

   _____

4. Are RAID 5 volumes supported under Windows XP Professional?

   _____

   _____

5. How can you set a quota limit for a particular user on Windows XP Professional?

   _____

   _____

# KEY TERM QUIZ

Use the following vocabulary terms to complete the sentences below. Not all of the terms will be used.

    basic disk

    compression

    dynamic disk

    encryption

    FAT

    FAT32

    NTFS

    RAID 5 volume

    simple volume

    spanned volume

    quota entry

1.  The _____ file system supports file-level security, compression, encryption, and disk quotas.

2.  Using _____ on files, folders, and programs reduces their size and the amount of space that they use on storage devices.

3.  _____ is a fault-tolerant volume with data and parity striped intermittently across three or more physical disks.

4.  _____ support the ability to create, extend, and manage volumes.

5.  _____ is the operating system of choice for Windows 95b, Windows 98, and Windows Me operating systems.

## LAB WRAP-UP

You should now be familiar with the tasks that are often done before a user starts to create and manage data on a Windows XP Professional computer. You should be familiar with the file systems, disk types, and storage-limit features that are supported by Windows XP Professional.

# LAB SOLUTIONS FOR CHAPTER 7

In this section, you'll find solutions to the lab exercises, lab analysis test, and key term quiz.

## Lab Solution 7.01

Your recommendation to Connor in regard to the file system on his shared computer should have looked something like the approach described here.

**Step 1.** One way to create the Connor's Files folder is to right-click the NTFS-formatted drive and select New | Folder from the menu. Right-click the Connor's Files folder, and select Properties. Figure 7-2 shows the Properties dialog for the folder.

**Step 2.** Figure 7-3 shows the Advanced Attributes dialog. Selecting Encrypt Contents To Secure Data will help prevent Connor's brother from reading Connor's files.

**FIGURE 7-2**

Viewing the folder properties for Connor's Files

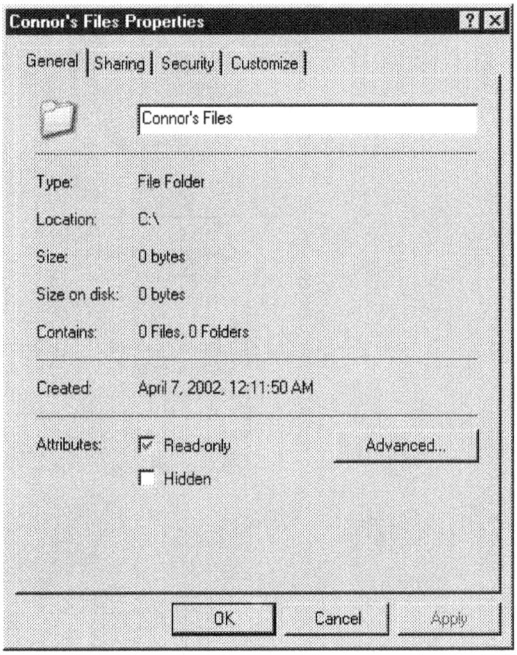

**FIGURE 7-3**

Choosing
to encrypt files
at the Advanced
Attributes dialog

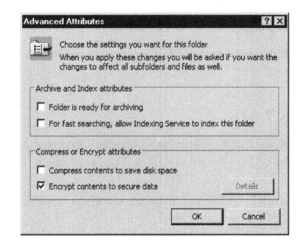

**Step 3.** From the Tools menu in Windows Explorer, select Folder Options. Select the View tab. Scroll to and clear Use Simple File Sharing (Recommended) from the Advanced Settings list (Figure 7-4). Click OK.

**FIGURE 7-4**

Disabling simple
file sharing for a
folder

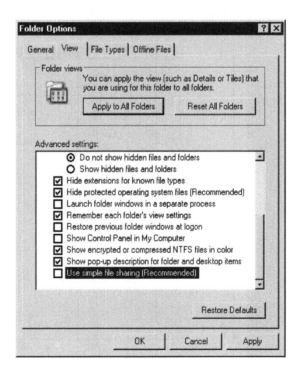

**FIGURE 7-5**

Reviewing the
options on the
Security tab
of the folder
Properties dialog

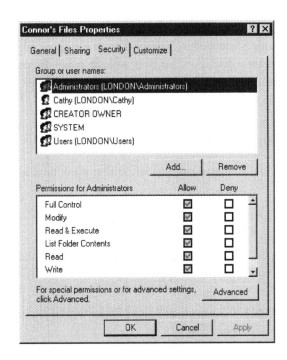

**Step 4.** Right-click Connor's Files, and choose Properties. Figure 7-5 shows the newly added Security tab. Options on that tab offer the ability to configure NTFS security for the folder. A Security tab will also be available to provide file-level security for all files that are created within the folder. Connor can use those options to prevent his brother from accessing the entire folder or individual files within the folder.

**Step 5.** FAT32 does not support file-level security or encryption. Connor should implement the NTFS file system, because it provides support for file encryption and file security, thereby protecting his files from access by his brother.

## Lab Solution 7.02

Here's the detail of your solution to help Lisa create spanned volumes.

**Step 1.** Disk 0 on Lisa's computer is shown as a basic disk. A basic disk supports partitions rather than volumes. To provide support for creating volumes on the disk, you need to convert it into a dynamic disk. However, Lisa's disk has already been divided into two partitions. The partitioning prevents Lisa from converting to a dynamic disk. For Lisa to be able to make the conversion, her disk would have to contain a single NTFS partition with additional free space. Only then will she be able to create volumes on the disk.

**Step 2.** To create a spanned volume on Disk 0, Lisa would have to

1. Re-partition the disk so that it contains a single partition with additional free/unallocated space.
2. Convert the basic disk to dynamic disk by right-clicking Disk 0 and choosing the appropriate option from the menu.
3. Right-click the free/unallocated space and use the New Volume wizard to create a new spanned volume.

**Step 3.** Answers will vary. Disks will be basic or dynamic, with one or more partitions or volumes.

**Step 4.** Answers will vary. Support for creating spanned volumes will depend on whether the disk is basic or dynamic and whether free/unallocated space is available.

## Lab Solution 7.03

Your solution for cutting Mike's disk quota to 100MB should resemble the one described here.

**Step 1.** Double-click My Computer. Right-click the NTFS-formatted drive, and select Properties. Click the Quota tab. (Figure 7-6 shows the Quota tab for an NTFS-formatted D: drive.)

**Step 2.** Figure 7-7 shows how to configure the defined quota limits for all users.

**Step 3.** Click the Quota Entries button. From the Quota menu, select New Quota Entry. Click Advanced, and then Find Now. Select the Mike user account

Lab Solutions for Chapter 7 **137**

**FIGURE 7-6**

Viewing the Quota
tab before any
quotas are set

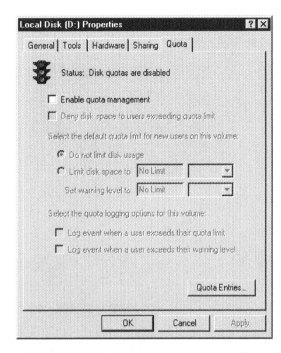

**FIGURE 7-7**

Setting a general
disk quota
for all users
of a computer

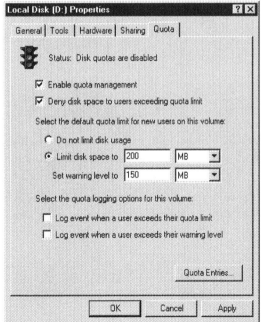

from the list of users, and click OK. The Select Users window opens with the Mike account selected:

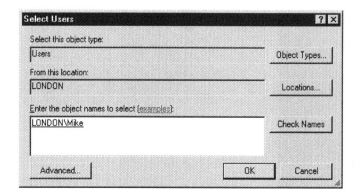

**Step 4.** Select Limit Space To, and configure the quota limit and warning level. Here is how the quota limits for Mike's user account should be configured:

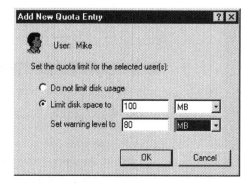

**Step 5.** If the quota limit is functioning properly, the reported free space for Mike's NTFS-formatted drive will indicate the quota limit that you established in step 4.

**Step 6.** You should be prevented from copying the 110MB of data to the NTFS-formatted drive owing to the quota limit that you established during the lab.

# ANSWERS TO LAB ANALYSIS TEST

1. These are the primary features of the NTFS file system:

   ■ **NTFS security**   You can individually configure files and folders with their own security features. You can also create individual security settings for users.

   ■ **Encryption**   You can encrypt a folder so that it cannot be read by someone else, and yet you can continue to use the data in that folder normally.

   ■ **Compression**   Using compression, you can reduce the amount of disk space needed to store data, while you continue to use the data as you normally would.

   ■ **Logging**   NTFS maintains a disk log that holds information about the functioning of the NTFS file system. In the event of a hard disk crash, the log can be helpful in recovering and repairing the data.

   ■ **Unlimited storage space**   An NTFS-formatted drive has no size limit.

2. Dynamic disks are capable of displaying several different states:

   ■ **Online**   The disk is online and functioning with no errors.

   ■ **Online (Errors)**   The disk is online, but some errors have occurred.

   ■ **Offline**   The disk is not accessible. The problem may be corruption or an I/O difficulty.

   ■ **Missing**   The disk is inaccessible or disconnected, or has become unreadable owing to corruption.

   ■ **Initializing**   The Initializing message occurs when the disk is temporarily unavailable owing to conversion to dynamic state.

   ■ **Not Initialized**   The Not Initialized message occurs when the disk lacks a valid signature (such as when you install a new disk).

   ■ **Foreign**   A disk is shown with the Foreign status when a physical dynamic disk is moved from a Windows 2000/XP Professional computer to another Windows 2000/XP Professional computer.

   ■ **Unreadable**   The Unreadable status appears when I/O errors prevent the disk from being read.

   ■ **No Media**   The No Media status appears when no media is currently inserted in a removable drive.

3. To extend the simple volume on a dynamic disk, you must select another area of free space on the same disk to enlarge the existing volume.

4. Raid 5 volumes are not supported under Windows XP Professional.

5. To set a quota for a particular user on Windows XP Professional, you must configure a quota entry for that user. In the quota entry, you must specify the limit and the warnings that you want to implement.

## ANSWERS TO KEY TERM QUIZ

1. NTFS

2. compression

3. RAID 5 volume

4. dynamic disks

5. FAT32

MICROSOFT CERTIFIED SYSTEMS ENGINEER

# 8

# Configuring and Managing Windows XP Printing and Faxing

## LAB EXERCISES

8.01 Installing and Managing a Local Printer

8.02 Installing and Connecting to an Internet Printer

8.03 Managing Printers and Print Jobs

8.04 Configuring and Troubleshooting Fax Support

■ Lab Analysis Test

■ Key Term Quiz

■ Lab Wrap-Up

■ Lab Solutions

This chapter examines the support that Windows XP Professional provides for the use of printers. You will practice installing, configuring, and troubleshooting printers and printer access. You will install and manage a local printer and work with network printers across the Internet. Additionally, you will establish printer security through the use of NTFS printer permissions. You will also examine the task of managing printers and print jobs. Finally, you will examine the new Fax console provided by Windows XP Professional. Using the Fax console, you can easily send, receive, and manage faxes.

If you are considering a career in IT support, you will most likely encounter all of these hands-on tasks in your future with Windows XP Professional.

**LAB EXERCISE 8.01**

# Installing and Managing a Local Printer          15 Minutes

Mike has asked you to install a printer in his office. He wants the printer to be solely for his use, preventing all other users from accessing the device. He has stated that he wants to print all documents in black ink. Mike also wants to be able to manage the print jobs that he sends to the printer. You want to ensure that you can also manage the printer in case of future technical problems. You choose to install a local printer on Mike's Windows XP Professional computer, and you configure the necessary NTFS printer permissions.

## Learning Objectives

In this lab, you install and configure a local printer on a Windows XP Professional computer. At the end of the lab, you'll be able to

- Install a local printer.
- Configure printing preferences.
- Configure NTFS printer permissions.

## Lab Materials and Setup

The materials you need for this lab are

- Pencil and paper
- Computer with Windows XP Professional installed
- NTFS partition on which to install a local printer

## Getting Down to Business

In this lab, you'll apply the knowledge that you acquired in the *MCSE Windows XP Professional Study Guide* to install a local printer on your Windows XP Professional computer.

**lab**
**Ⓗint** *A physical print device is not required for this lab. You will use the printer software included with Windows XP Professional to create the local printer.*

**Step 1.** At the Windows XP Professional computer, log on as Administrator. Browse to the Printers and Faxes folder and install a local printer with these settings:

| | |
|---|---|
| **Printer type** | Local printer (no automatic detection) |
| **Printer port** | LPT1 |
| **Printer manufacturer and model** | HP 2500C Series |
| **Default printer** | Yes |
| **Shared printer** | No |
| **Print test page** | No |

**lab**
**Ⓗint** *When installing a physical Plug and Play device, an administrator may choose to have the Windows XP Professional computer detect the device to ensure that the computer recognizes it. An administrator may also choose to print a test page to ensure that the print device is connected and working properly. Neither task is necessary for the purposes of this lab.*

**Step 2.** Open the Properties sheet for the HP 2500C Series printer that you just installed, and select the Security tab. What are the default NTFS printer permissions for the new printer?

_____

_____

**Step 3.** Configure the printer permissions to accommodate Mike's requests as stated in the scenario. Use the Mike user account that you created in an earlier lab. (If the Mike account has been deleted, you can re-create the account at the Computer Management | Local Users and Groups console.)

lab
ⓗint

*Ensure that you remove unnecessary permissions. Also remember to retain default permissions that allow you to manage the printer.*

**Step 4.** Configure the Printing Preferences for the new printer to suit Mike's request that all documents be printed with black ink. Save the configuration and close all open windows.

lab
ⓦarning

*Do not delete the HP 2500C Series printer; you will need it for future labs.*

**LAB EXERCISE 8.02**

# Installing and Connecting to an Internet Printer

15 Minutes

Dean wants to connect to the HP 2500C Series printer that you installed on your Windows XP Professional computer. He has asked for your help in accomplishing that task. He wants to learn about connecting to a printer through a web browser. He also wants you to teach him the various ways that he can connect to the printer to send print jobs.

## Learning Objectives

In this lab, you install and connect to an Internet printer. At the end of the lab, you'll be able to

- Install an Internet printer over a network.
- View Internet printers through a browser.
- Connect to an Internet printer.

## Lab Materials and Setup

The materials you need for this lab are

- Pencil and paper
- Computer A and computer B—two local network computers with Windows XP Professional installed
- HP 2500C Series local printer installed on computer A (from lab 8.01)
- Web browser (Internet Explorer 4.0 or later) installed on computer B
- Windows XP Professional CD

## Getting Down to Business

The steps that follow guide you in installing and connecting to an Internet printer. You will have to apply the knowledge you acquired in the *MCSE Windows XP Professional Study Guide* to complete the lab.

**Step 1.** On computer A, at the Add Or Remove Programs dialog, install the Windows XP component called Internet Information Services (IIS).

On computer A, share the HP 2500C Series printer that you created in lab 8.01. Give it the share name **HP2500CS**.

On computer B, log on as Administrator. Using the Add Printer wizard, choose to add a network printer. Choose to connect to a printer on the Internet, and specify the UNC path of the HP 2500C Series printer that you created on computer A (your Windows XP Professional computer) in lab 8.01. Ensure that the Internet printer object was created.

**Step 2.** At your web browser on computer B, enter the URL for the location of the printer that you just added. The browser should list the Internet printer. Once you locate the printer, if you were to click Connect, what would be the result of your actions on computer B?

_____

_____

**Step 3.** If you do not know the name of a printer to which you would like to connect, what URL would show you the names of all the printers on a particular computer?

_____

_____

**Step 4.** If Dean did not want to connect to the remote printer through a URL, how else might he configure the connection?

_____

_____

## LAB EXERCISE 8.03

# Managing Printers and Print Jobs

**30 Minutes**

Cathy has tried to print to Mike's HP2500CS Internet printer. Her payroll document failed to print and she has asked for your help in troubleshooting the problem. She is unsure if the problem was caused by hardware or software. She is also unfamiliar with where to look for the status of her print job and how to enable her document to print.

## Learning Objectives

In this lab, you manage a printer, and you troubleshoot a print-job problem. At the end of the lab, you'll be able to

- Configure printer settings.
- Troubleshoot a printing problem.
- Manage a printer.

## Lab Materials and Setup

For this lab exercise, you'll need

- Pencil and paper
- Computer A and computer B—two local network computers with Windows XP Professional installed
- HP 2500C Series local printer installed on computer A (from lab 8.01)

## Getting Down to Business

To solve Cathy's problem, use this procedure.

**Step 1.** Where can Cathy view the status of her print job? Give a brief answer in the space provided.

_____

_____

**Step 2.** At computer B, log on as Administrator. Create a document in Notepad called **Payroll**, and attempt to print the document using the printer shared as HP2500CS.
   View the print status of document Payroll. Note the status in the space provided. Why would your print job have that status?

_____

_____

**Step 3.** What troubleshooting options are available to Cathy for managing documents, once she views the status of her print job? From the printer queue on computer B, view the available options for managing the Payroll document that you attempted to print. List them in the space provided.

_____

_____

**Step 4.** Given the information provided in the scenario, can you tell what is preventing Cathy's document from printing? What hardware troubleshooting options should you consider when managing the printer?

_____

_____

**LAB EXERCISE 8.04**

# Configuring and Troubleshooting Fax Support

**30 Minutes**

Jennifer has started a new home-based business called Smith Enterprises. She wants to use her Windows XP Professional computer to send and receive faxes. She has only a single phone line. She therefore wants to manually answer all calls so that she can distinguish incoming fax calls from other phone calls. She wants her incoming fax messages to be saved in her My Documents folder and in the Inbox archive of her Fax console. Finally, she wants sound notification when fax errors are detected, with the failed faxes being automatically deleted after three days.

## Learning Objectives

Although peripherals come in all shapes, sizes, and technologies, you can apply a standard set of procedures to the installation and configuration of peripherals. At the end of the lab, you'll be able to

- Install the Windows component called Fax Services.
- Configure the Fax console.

## Lab Materials and Setup

For this lab exercise, you'll need

- Computer with Windows XP Professional installed
- Fax/modem installed

## Getting Down to Business

In the lab that follows, you have to apply the knowledge that you acquired in the *MCSE Windows XP Professional Study Guide* for installing and configuring fax services on your Windows XP Professional computer.

*If you do not have a fax/modem installed on your computer, you can use the Add Hardware wizard to install one.*

**Step 1.** Use Add Or Remove Programs to install the Fax Services component of Windows on your Windows XP Professional computer.

**Step 2.** Use the settings in the table that follows to configure the Fax console:

| | |
|---|---|
| **Full name** | Jennifer Smith |
| **Fax number** | 201-555-1111 |
| **E-mail address** | jsmith@smithenterprises.com |
| **Fax device** | Indicate the fax/modem on your computer |
| **Sending options** | Enable Send and Receive (manual answer) |
| **TSID** | 201-555-1111 |
| **CSID** | SmithEnterprises |

**Step 3.** At the Control Panel | Printers and Faxes folder, configure the Fax object to suit Jennifer's request for sound notification when errors are detected.

**Step 4.** At the Fax object, configure the cleanup settings so that failed faxes are automatically deleted after three days. Save all settings and close all open windows.

# LAB ANALYSIS TEST

1.  How does having a network adapter card installed in a network printer affect the options available for printing?

    _____

    _____

2.  If a user is accessing your shared Internet printer through a web browser, what options do they have in terms of managing documents?

    _____

    _____

3.  What option is available for troubleshooting communication problems with Windows XP Professional and older print devices?

    _____

    _____

4.  What additional security options does a fax object in the Printers and Faxes folder have?

    _____

    _____

5.  Can you connect to an Internet printer through the Netscape web browser?

    _____

    _____

# KEY TERM QUIZ

Use the following vocabulary terms to complete the sentences below. Not all of the terms will be used.

Graphical Device Interface (GDI)

Internet Information Services (IIS)

Internet Printing Protocol (IPP)

local printer

LPT port

network printer

print device

printer pool

printer priority

print processor

print queue

print spooler

TCP/IP port

1.  The _____ allows computers running Windows XP to print to a print device on the Internet.

2.  To configure a printer so that it can be accessed by URL, _____ must be installed on your Windows XP Professional computer.

3.  You must configure a(n) _____ if you want to control the order in which multiple printers attached to a single print device will print.

4.  A _____ is two or more identical print devices that function through one logical printer.

5.  A _____ is a logical port indicating the IP address of a network printer.

# LAB WRAP-UP

You should now be familiar with the various types of printers that Windows XP Professional supports, as well as with how to configure those printers and establish NTFS security for them. You should also be comfortable with the process of sharing a printer and working with a printer across a network and across the Internet. Finally, you should be familiar with the Fax console and the support for fax devices that Windows XP Professional provides.

# LAB SOLUTIONS FOR CHAPTER 8

In this section, you'll find solutions to the lab exercises, lab analysis test, and key term quiz.

## Lab Solution 8.01

You can meet all of Mike's needs (and your own) by configuring his printer as described here.

**Step 1.**    At the Printers and Faxes folder, use the Add Printer wizard to install the printer, using the specified criteria.

Click Next to bypass the splash screen. At the Local Or Network Printer window, choose the Local Printer option, and clear the check box for automatic detection. Click Next.

At the Select A Printer Port window, select Use The Following Port, and choose LPT1: in the drop-down list. Click Next.

At the Install Printer Software window, select HP in the Manufacturer list, and HP 2500C Series in the Printers list. Click Next.

At the Name Your Printer screen, accept the default name HP 2500C Series, and ensure that you choose Yes to make the new printer the default printer. Click Next.

At the Printer Sharing window, disable sharing by choosing Do Not Share This Printer. Click Next.

At the Print Test Page window, choose No, and click Next.

Review the printer settings, and click Finish.

**Step 2.**    The default permissions for the newly created printer are

- Administrators group—Print, Manage Printers, Manage Documents
- Creator/Owner—Manage Documents
- Everyone—Print
- Power Users—Print, Manage Printers, Manage Documents

**Step 3.**    The newly configured permissions for the printer should look like this:

- Administrators group—Print, Manage Printers, Manage Documents
- Mike user account—Print, Manage Documents

The Print permission is automatically selected with the Manage Printers permission. The Print permission is needed to be able to print a test page while managing the printer. That permission is therefore granted to the Administrators group, even though Mike has requested that he be the only person able to print to the printer.

**Step 4.** Go to the Paper/Quality tab of the HP 2500C Series Printing Preferences dialog, and select the Black & White option (Figure 8-1) so that all print jobs will print with black ink.

## Lab Solution 8.02

Your solution to help Dean connect to the HP 2500C Series printer on your Windows XP Professional should resemble the solution described here.

**Step 1.** At the Control Panel on computer A, open Add Or Remove Programs, and choose to install the Internet Information Services (IIS) component of Windows XP. Insert the Windows XP Professional CD into the CD drive when prompted. Remove the CD when you are done.

Then, right-click the HP 2500C Series printer, choose Properties, and select the Sharing tab in the Properties dialog. Give the printer the share name **HP2500CS**.

**FIGURE 8-1**

Choosing
Black & White
as the default
for all print jobs

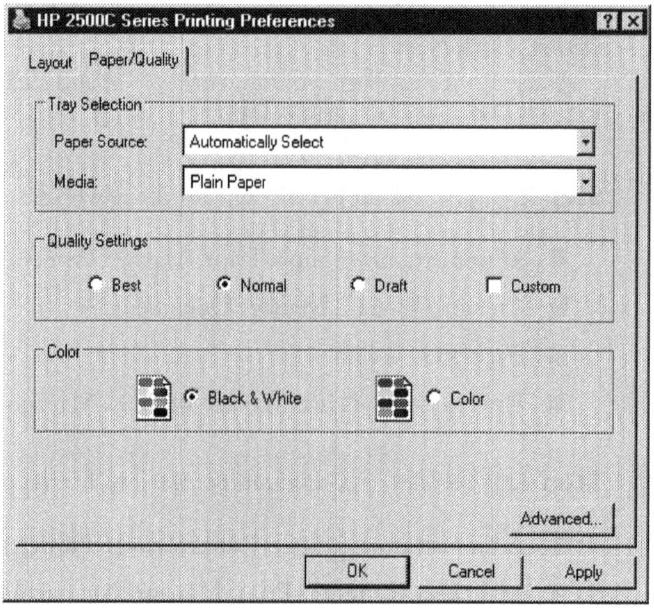

**FIGURE 8-2**

Configuring
the path to an
Internet printer

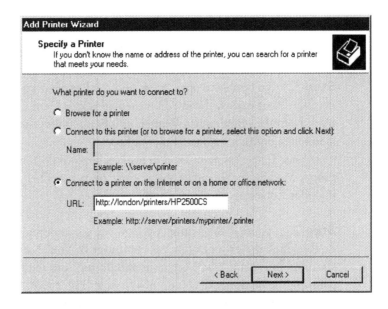

At computer B, configure the path to the Internet printer on computer A. (Figure 8-2 shows a sample path.)

Click Next, and click Finish to create the printer.

**Step 2.** When you click Connect in the browser for the Internet printer, Windows XP copies the necessary drivers, and the new printer appears in your Printers and Faxes folder. This simple method of using a browser to access an Internet printer is an alternative to the Add Printer wizard.

**Step 3.** If you do not know the name of a printer that you want to connect to, you can type the URL for the server that on which the printer is located. The URL http://*servername*/printers shows a list of the print devices available on the specified server.

**Step 4.** To connect to the remote HP 2500C Series printer other than through a URL, Dean would have to use the Add Printer wizard to create a network printer on computer B, either specifying the UNC path of the printer, or browsing to the location of the printer on computer A.

## Lab Solution 8.03

Clearing up Cathy's print problem involves the steps described here.

**Step 1.** To be able to open, view, and modify the print queue, you must have the necessary permissions. If you don't, then an Access Denied message appears when you try to open the printer in the Printers and Faxes folder, and you will not see a printer icon in the notification area of the Taskbar.

Because Cathy has permission to manage her own documents in the HP2500CS printer window, she should be able to view the status of her print job by double-clicking the printer object in the Printers and Faxes folder.

**Step 2.** To view the printer window for the Internet printer HP2500CS, double-click the printer object at computer B. You should be able to view the status of your print job. The status should indicate that an error occurred when printing the document. You do not have an HP 2500C Series print device attached to your computer; the print job has therefore failed.

**Step 3.** It is important to note that, because Cathy has the ability to manage her own documents in the printer queue, she would be able to see her documents there and delete them if necessary. If the queue contained multiple documents, an Administrator could also choose to cancel all documents, change the priority of documents in the queue, or configure a schedule for a particular print job.

**Step 4.** The scenario does not provide enough information to indicate what is preventing Cathy's document from printing. Cathy should start by checking that the print device is powered on and that all cables are properly connected. She should check to see that the ink and paper levels are adequate to print the document and that she can access the printer across the network. Cathy should also check her printer drivers and port settings.

## Lab Solution 8.04

Here's how to configure Jennifer's fax setup to meet her needs.

**Step 1.** Open the Control Panel, and run Add Or Remove Programs, choosing to install the Fax Services component of Windows XP Professional. Once installation is complete, the Fax console should appear in the Programs | Accessories | Communications | Fax menu.

**Step 2.** Choose Programs | Accessories | Communications | Fax | Fax Console to launch the Fax console. Configure the console with Jennifer's business information as shown in Figure 8-3. Click Next.

At the Select Device for Sending or Receiving Faxes screen, choose both Enable Send and Enable Receive. Choose the manual answer option for receiving. Click Next.

At the Transmitting Subscriber Identification (TSID) screen, configure the Smith Enterprises ID as shown in Figure 8-4. Click Next.

At the Called Subscriber Identification (CSID) screen, configure the Smith Enterprises ID as shown in Figure 8-5. Click Next.

At the Routing Options screen, choose to store received faxes in the My Documents folder. Click Next. Review the configuration settings, and then click Finish.

**Step 3.** At the Printers and Faxes folder, you should have opened the Fax object. At the Tracking tab, you should have selected the Configure Sound Settings button. The default sound settings should indicate that all sounds are enabled. You should

FIGURE 8-4

Configuring
the transmitting
subscriber ID in
the Fax console

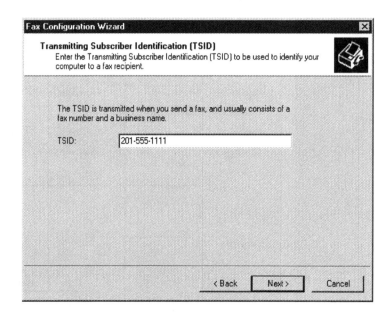

FIGURE 8-5

Configuring
the called
subscriber ID
in the Fax
console

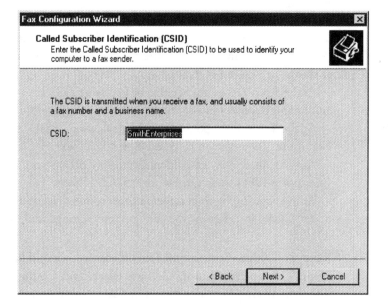

have configured the setting only to play a sound when an error is detected. All other settings should be cleared.

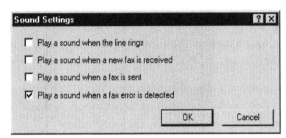

**Step 4.** At the Printers and Faxes folder, double-click the Fax object. Choose Properties, and click the Cleanup tab. Configure the cleanup settings to delete failed faxes after three days:

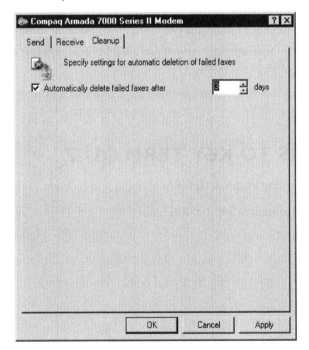

Accept the setting and close all open windows.

## ANSWERS TO LAB ANALYSIS TEST

1.  If a network printer has a network adapter card, you can choose to add a TCP/IP port to the printer. Using the TCP/IP port, your computer can print to the IP port on the network adapter in the printer, assuming that you have permission to do so. The result is that your computer can send print jobs through TCP/IP directly to the network printer.

2.  When a user accesses a shared printer through a web browser, that user can delete owned documents if necessary. The Manage Documents permission is required for making changes affecting non-owned documents in the print queue.

3.  To troubleshoot communications or compatibility problems with Windows XP Professional and certain older print devices, you can open the Advanced tab of the printer's Properties dialog and clear the check box labeled Enable Advanced Printing Features. That action might help to resolve some of the problems.

4.  On a Windows XP Professional computer, the Fax Security tab in the fax Properties dialog provides a list of fax permissions. The available permissions are: Fax, Manage Fax Configuration, and Manage Fax Documents.

5.  The Netscape browser cannot be used to connect to an Internet printer. You must use Internet Explorer 4.0 or later to connect to Internet printers.

## ANSWERS TO KEY TERM QUIZ

1.  Internet Printing Protocol (IPP)

2.  Internet Information Services (IIS)

3.  printer priority

4.  printer pool

5.  TCP/IP port

# 9

# Resource
# Administration

This chapter looks at the ways in which Windows XP Professional can be used to share information. You will work with file and folder compression and see the effect on disk space and file access. You will learn how to implement file and folder management, and to configure NTFS security for resources. You will learn to share folders and files in a variety of ways, from sharing with users on the same computer, to sharing with remote users over a network. You will learn how you can use the Internet Information Services (IIS) console to configure a virtual directory for a web share. You will also configure offline files on your computer and work with the caching and synchronization of those files.

**LAB EXERCISE 9.01**

# Implementing File Compression

**30 Minutes**

Sanela is interested in learning about the file and folder compression feature offered by Windows XP Professional. She has asked you to demonstrate how to enable file compression. She is also interested in seeing how compression affects moving and copying compressed files on her computer.

## Learning Objectives

In this lab, you work with compressed files on an NTFS partition. At the end of the lab, you'll be able to

- Create and compress a folder on an NTFS partition.
- Apply compression to a file.
- Copy a compressed file.
- Move a compressed file.

## Lab Materials and Setup

The materials you need for this lab are

- Pencil and paper
- One computer with Windows XP Professional installed
- NTFS-formatted drive

## Getting Down to Business

The steps that follow guide you in implementing file compression. You will have to apply the knowledge that you acquired in the *MCSE Windows XP Professional Study Guide* to complete the lab.

**Step 1.** Log on to the Windows XP Professional computer as Administrator. In Windows Explorer, find the Folder options, and verify that compressed NTFS files will be shown in color.

**Step 2.** Create a new folder on the NTFS-formatted drive, and name it **Accounting**. Copy and paste the Mike folder from the Documents and Settings folder on the C: drive into the new Accounting folder.

lab
ⓗint
*You should have created the Mike profile folder in an earlier lab by logging onto the computer using the Mike user account. If the Mike profile folder does not exist, select another user or the All Users folder instead.*

**Step 3.** Open the Properties dialog for the Accounting folder. In the space provided here, note the size of the folder.

_____

_____

**Step 4.** Choose to compress the contents of the Accounting folder. Close the Accounting folder.

**Step 5.** When the Confirm Attribute Changes window opens, choose to apply compression to the Accounting folder, its subfolders, and all files. What happens to the Accounting folder?

_____

_____

**Step 6.** Re-open the Properties dialog for the Accounting folder. In the space provided, note the new size of the folder. How does the new size compare to the previous size?

_____

_____

**Step 7.** In the Accounting folder, create a text file called **Payroll**. Does the file inherit the compressed attributes of the folder? Briefly give a reason for your answer.

_____

_____

**Step 8.** Copy the Payroll file, and paste it to the NTFS-formatted drive. Does the Payroll file retain its attributes? Briefly give a reason for your answer. Delete the Payroll file.

_____

_____

**Step 9.** Move the Payroll file from the Accounting folder to the C: drive. Does the file retain its attributes? Briefly give a reason for your answer.

_____

_____

**Step 10.** Remove the compression attribute from the Accounting folder and all its subfolders. (Do not delete the Accounting folder; you need it for a future lab.)

**LAB EXERCISE 9.02**

# Working with Shared Folders

**30 Minutes**

Cathy shares a computer with other part-time employees at the research company where she works. Cathy wants to make sure that all users of that computer have access to the Business folder that currently exists in her My Documents folder. She also wants to make her Data folder available to all other users and Administrators who belong to the local workgroup and who sit at other Windows XP Professional computers.

## Learning Objectives

In this lab, you work with shared folders in Windows XP Professional. At the end of the lab, you'll be able to

- Share a folder with local sharing and security for users on the same computer.
- Share a folder with network sharing and security for computers on the same network.
- Verify the sharing of folders locally and over the network.

## Lab Materials and Setup

The materials you need for this lab are

- Pencil and paper
- Computer A and computer B—local network computers with Windows XP Professional installed

## Getting Down to Business

To set up Cathy's computer for the sharing scheme she wants, here is how to proceed.

**Step 1.**   Log on to computer A as Administrator. Create a user named **Cathy** with a password of **2002JKL**. Create the **Mike** user account if it does not already exist. Log off the computer.

**Step 2.**   Log on to computer A as Cathy, using the assigned password. Open the My Documents folder, and create a new folder called **Data**. Create a second folder called **Business**. Once you have created the Business folder, share it with other users of the current computer..

**Step 3.**   Verify that the Business folder has been shared. Close all open windows, and log off.

**Step 4.** Log on to computer A as Mike, using a blank password. Double-click the My Computer object on the desktop. Double-click the Shared Documents folder. Do you have access to the folder? Why or why not? Log off computer A.

_____

_____

**Step 5.** Log on to computer A as Cathy, using the assigned password. Arrange for the Data folder to be shared by other network users, but prevent those users from changing the files in the folder.

**Step 6.** Verify that the Data folder appears as a shared folder on the local computer.

**Step 7.** At computer B, log on as Administrator. Use My Network Places to browse to the Data folder on computer A.

Can you open the folder? Can you create a new text document in the Data folder? Why or why not?

Close all open windows. Log off both computers.

## LAB EXERCISE 9.03

# Configuring Advanced Security

**30 Minutes**

Mike wants to make sure that only he and the local Administrators can access the Accounting folder on his Windows XP Professional computer. He wants to remove any unnecessary permissions that propagate to the Accounting folder from a parent object. He wants to ensure that he and the local Administrators are granted Full Control over the Accounting folder but no other users, including his assistant Cheryl, are able to access the folder.

## Learning Objectives

In this lab, you implement advanced security on an NTFS drive. At the end of the lab, you'll be able to

- Implement advanced security.
- Assign NTFS permissions to users and group accounts.
- View the effects of advanced security on resource access.

## Lab Materials and Setup

The materials you need for this lab are

- Pencil and paper
- Computer with Windows XP Professional installed
- NTFS partition

## Getting Down to Business

To help Mike keep his Accounting folder private, here's how to proceed:

**Step 1.** Log on to the Windows XP Professional computer as Administrator. View the tabs on the Properties dialog for the Accounting folder that you created in a previous lab. Close the Accounting folder. Using the Control Panel | Folder Options object, ensure that advanced security can be set up for the Accounting folder. Re-open the Accounting folder properties. How have the tabs changed?

_____

_____

**Step 2.** Still at the Security tab of Properties dialog for the Accounting folder, what are the default permissions for the folder?

_____

_____

**Step 3.** Try to remove the Users account. In the space provided, note the result.

_____

_____

**Step 4.** Remove the inherited permissions from the Users group. Read the security message that appears, and click Remove. What happens to all the permission entries?

_____

_____

lab
**Warning**

*An error message will appear stating that you have denied everyone access to the Accounting folder. Only the owner can change permissions. You must agree with the message to be able to continue.*

**Step 5.** Grant to the Administrators group Full Control over the Accounting folder.

**Step 6.** Grant the Mike account Full Control over the Accounting folder.

**Step 7.** Verify that the desired permissions have been applied to the Accounting folder, and all its subfolders and files.

**Step 8.** At the Permissions tab in the Advanced Security Settings dialog for folder Accounting, double-click the Mike user account. Verify that Mike's effective permissions are applied to the Accounting folder and all its subfolders and files. Change the setting so that Mike's effective permissions apply to only the Accounting folder and all its subfolders.

**Step 9.** Ensure that the Cheryl user account appears in the Users container. If the Cheryl user account is not there, create the account with a blank password. Close all windows and log off the computer.

**Step 10.** Log on to the computer using the Cheryl account. Browse to the Accounting folder, and attempt to open it. Were you able to access the folder? Why or why not?

_____

_____

**LAB EXERCISE 9.04**

# Examining Combined NTFS and Shared Folder Permissions

**30 Minutes**

Cathy wants to make sure that all users who log on locally to her shared Windows XP Professional computer have access to the Management folder that currently exists on an NTFS-formatted drive. She wants also to ensure that all Managers who log on locally can access the file, but that any Manager who logs on over the network will be denied access.

She also wants Administrators who log on locally to be able to administer the folder. Cathy wants to combine shared permissions with NTFS advanced security permissions to achieve her goal.

## Learning Objectives

In this lab, you configure both shared and NTFS permissions for a folder on a Windows XP Professional computer. At the end of the lab, you'll be able to

- Share a folder with network sharing and security for computers on the same network.
- Implement NTFS permissions on a folder.
- Verify the effect of combined permissions on a folder over the network.

## Lab Materials and Setup

The materials you need for this lab are

- Pencil and paper
- Windows XP Professional computer

## Getting Down to Business

To set up the appropriate permissions for Cathy's management folder, use the procedure described here.

**Step 1.** Log on to the computer as Administrator, and create a local security group called Managers. Add the Mike account to the group. Log off the computer.

**Step 2.** Log back on to the computer as Cathy, using the assigned password, 2002JKL. At the NTFS-formatted drive, create a new folder called **Management**. Inside the folder, create a text document called **Private File**.

**Step 3.** Share the Management folder on the network, but deny access to the Managers security group. Clear all permission check boxes for the Everyone group.

**Step 4.** Select the Security tab. To the Managers security group, give the permissions Read And Execute, List Folder Contents, and Read. Assign Full Control to the Administrators group. Clear all the permissions check boxes for the Everyone group.

**Step 5.** Log on to the computer as Mike. Try to access the Private File text file through the Management folder. Were you able to access the file? Give reasons for your answer.

_____

_____

**Step 6.** Still logged in as Mike, try to access Private File from the Management share in My Network Places. Were you able to access the file? Give reasons for your answer.

_____

_____

**LAB EXERCISE 9.05**

# Configuring a Web Share

**30 Minutes**

Mike would like to configure his Windows XP Professional computer to host a web page that he wants to share with other users on the local intranet. He wants to make this resource available to users without requiring them to enter a username and password. He has asked for your help in setting up a virtual directory with the Internet Information Services (IIS) component of Windows XP Professional.

## Learning Objectives

In this lab, you use Internet Information Services to set up a virtual directory. At the end of the lab, you'll be able to

- Install the Internet Information Services component of Windows XP Professional.

- Create a virtual directory.

- Configure security on a virtual directory.

## Lab Materials and Setup

For this lab exercise, you'll need

- Pencil and paper
- Computer with Windows XP Professional installed

## Getting Down to Business

Sharing web-based resources is becoming more common in networked environments. Here's how to proceed.

**Step 1.** Log on to the Windows XP Professional computer as Administrator. Open the IIS console. Expand Web Sites, and select the Default Web Site object.

**Step 2.** Start the Virtual Directory Creation wizard. After bypassing the splash screen, enter the name **Mike's Web Site** in the Virtual Directory Alias window.

**Step 3.** For Web Site Content Directory, enter **C:\Documents and Settings\ Mike\My Documents** as the directory that contains the content.

**lab Hint** *The Mike profile folder should appear in the Documents And Settings folder, because you placed it there in a previous lab. If the profile folder is not present, select another user profile folder in this step.*

**Step 4.** In the Access Permissions window, verify that Read and Run Scripts permissions are selected. Complete the wizard.

**Step 5.** Check the default authentication method for the Mike's Web Site object. What is the authentication method, and why is it selected as the default?

_____

_____

## LAB EXERCISE 9.06

# Configuring Offline Files

**45 Minutes**

Samuel wants to learn how to make his computer available for offline file use. He has asked you to demonstrate how to create offline files, and how to cache and synchronize offline files on his Windows XP Professional computer.

## Learning Objectives

In this lab, you configure a computer to handle offline files. At the end of the lab, you'll be able to

- Prepare a computer for offline file use.
- Create an offline file.
- Configure caching options on a shared folder.
- Modify an offline file.
- Synchronize an offline file.

## Lab Materials and Setup

For this lab exercise, you'll need

- Pencil and paper
- Computer A and computer B—local network computers with Windows XP Professional installed

## Getting Down to Business

Use this procedure to show Samuel how to manage offline files.

**Step 1.** Log on to computer B as Administrator. Enable Offline Files for all folders, and verify that all offline files will be synchronized before logging off.

**Step 2.** Log on to computer A as Administrator. Give the Everyone group the Full Control permission over the Data folder that you previously created in Shared Folders.

**Step 3.** Verify that manual caching of documents is selected.

**Step 4.** On computer B, create a user account named **John**. Log off as Administrator.

**Step 5.** Log on to computer B as John. In the Data folder, create a new text document called **Offline Test**.

**Step 6.** Open the Offline Test text document, and type **This is a test**. Save and close the text document. Arrange for the Offline Test text document to be available for offline access when you are not connected to the network.

**Step 7.** Verify that automatic synchronization during log on and log off is off, but choose to enable reminders and to create a shortcut to the Offline Files folder on the Desktop.

**lab**
**Hint** *You should see synchronization take place. The offline symbol (two arrows) should appear on the Offline file.*

**Step 8.** At the Desktop on computer B, create an offline version of the Offline Test text document.

**Step 9.** Using the Network Connections menu, take computer B off the network.

**lab**
**Hint** *It takes a few seconds for the computer to be removed from the network. Ensure that the connection is disabled before you continue. To indicate that the network is not available, an Offline Files icon appears in the Taskbar notification area.*

**Step 10.** Open the Offline Test document. Try to change the document and save the changes. Close the document.

**Step 11.**  Using the Offline Files Status icon on the Taskbar, choose Work Online Without Synchronizing Changes from the Offline File Status dialog box. Re-open the Offline Test document. Does the document have the changes that you added? Briefly give a reason for your answer.

_____

_____

**Step 12.**  Re-enable your local area connection. What happens to the offline files after you reconnect to the local network? At the View tab in Control Panel | Folder Options, disable offline files.

_____

_____

# LAB ANALYSIS TEST

1. When share-level permissions and NTFS permissions are combined, what is the effect on the permissions that the user actually receives?

   _____

   _____

2. A user has the NTFS permission Write and the share-level permission Full Control on a particular share. What is the user's effective permission?

   _____

   _____

3. If you copy a compressed file to a folder that is not compressed, does the file retain its compression status? Why or why not? If a compressed file is moved to a folder that is not compressed, does it retain its compression status?

   _____

   _____

4. Are you able to use offline files on a Windows XP Professional computer that is configured for fast-user switching?

   _____

   _____

5. What is the purpose of the Internet Information Services component in Windows XP Professional?

   _____

   _____

# KEY TERM QUIZ

Use the following vocabulary terms to complete the sentences below. Not all of the terms will be used.

anonymous authentication

automatic caching of documents

compact.exe

compression

file encryption

file synchronization

Integrated Windows Authentication

manual caching of documents

NTFS permissions

Offline Files wizard

share-level permission

Synchronization tool

virtual directory

1. The default authentication method for a new virtual directory in IIS is _____ .

2. You can configure the _____ to create an Offline Files folder on the Desktop.

3. With _____ , users must specify the files that they want to make available when working offline.

4. Storing data in a format that requires less space than usual is known as _____ .

5. You can apply _____ to implement advanced security for users on the local computer.

# LAB WRAP-UP

You should now be familiar with configuring compression on folders, sharing files and folders on a local network, and setting NTFS permissions on resources. Additionally, you should know how to configure a virtual directory using the Internet Information Services console. Finally, you should be comfortable with configuring your computer to use offline files.

# LAB SOLUTIONS FOR CHAPTER 9

In this section, you'll find solutions to the lab exercises, lab analysis test, and key term quiz.

## Lab Solution 9.01

Your demonstration to Sanela of file and folder compression should have proceeded like the one described here.

**Step 1.** After logging on as Administrator, open Windows Explorer. From the Tools menu, select Folder Options. The View tab contains the option for color display of encrypted compressed NTFS files. Ensure that Show Encrypted Or Compressed NTFS Files In Color is selected:

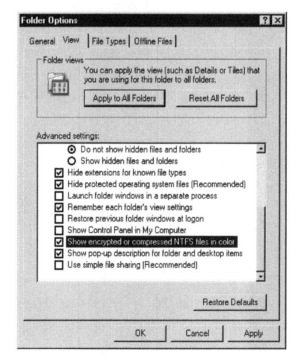

Click OK.

**Step 2.** At the Windows Explorer window, select the NTFS-formatted drive. On the NTFS drive, create a new folder, and give it the name **Accounting**. Expand the Documents and Settings folder on the C: drive. Select the Mike folder. Copy and paste the Mike folder into the new Accounting folder. The Mike folder should become a subfolder of the Accounting folder on the NTFS-formatted drive:

**Step 3.**   Right-click the Accounting folder, and select Properties from the pop-up menu. In the Properties dialog, find and note the size of the folder. Answers will vary, because the Accounting folder will vary in size with the size of the Mike profile. Leave the Properties dialog open for the next step.

**Step 4.**   Click the General tab in the Properties dialog for the Accounting folder. Click the Advanced button. Choose Compress Contents To Save Disk Space. Click OK. Click OK to close the Properties dialog.

**Step 5.**   In the Confirm Attribute Changes window, choose to apply compression to the Accounting folder, its subfolders, and all files. Click OK. The Accounting folder should now appear with blue lettering, indicating that it is a compressed folder.

**Step 6.**   Right-click the Accounting folder, and choose Properties from the pop-up menu. Answers about the new size of the Accounting folder will vary. The compressed version of the folder should be smaller in size than the uncompressed version observed in step 3.

**Step 7.**   The newly created Payroll document inherits the compressed attribute because it was created inside an already-compressed folder.

**Step 8.** The Payroll document inherits the state of the location to which it is copied. In this case, you copied and pasted it to the NTFS-formatted drive, which is uncompressed. The Payroll document therefore becomes uncompressed.

**Step 9.** When moved from the Accounting folder on the NTFS-formatted drive to another location on the drive, the Payroll document retains the its current (compressed) state.

**Step 10.** Click the General tab in the Properties dialog for the Accounting folder. Click the Advanced button. Clear the compress option. Click OK. Click OK to close the Properties dialog. The Accounting folder should become uncompressed.

## Lab Solution 9.02

Here is how you would have helped Cathy to appropriately share her files and folders.

**Step 1.** Use the Computer Management administrative tool to create the Cathy user account (and the Mike user account, if necessary).

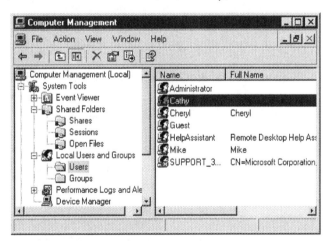

**Step 2.** Click and drag the Business folder to the Other Places heading inside the Shared Documents folder (to the left of the My Documents window).

**Step 3.** Click the Shared Documents link. The Shared Documents window should open, showing the Business folder inside. The Business folder is now available to all users of this Windows XP Professional computer.

**Step 4.** The Mike user account should be able to access the Business folder located within the Shared Documents folder, because you made it available to all users on the same Windows XP Professional computer.

**Step 5.** In the My Documents folder, right-click the Data folder. Select Sharing And Security from the pop-up menu. At the Sharing tab, select the Share This Folder On The Network check box. Clear the Allow Network Users To Change My Files check box (Figure 9-1). Click OK.

**Step 6.** Open the Computer Management administrative tool. Expand the Shared Folders object, and select the Shares object. The Data folder should appear within Shares in the Computer Management administrative tool:

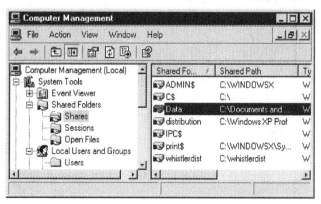

Configuring
network sharing
and security
for a folder

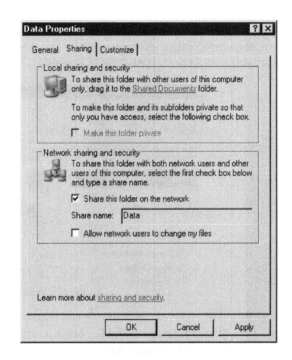

**Step 7.** Double-click My Network Places on the desktop. Browse to the Data folder on computer A, and attempt to open the folder. From computer B, you should be able to access the Data folder located on computer A. However, when you attempt to create a text document within the Data folder, you should receive an Access Is Denied error message, because you were not given permission to make changes to the Data folder.

## Lab Solution 9.03

Here's how you would have helped Mike to protect his sensitive information.

**Step 1.** At the Control Panel | Folder Options object, select the View tab. Clear the check box labelled Use Simple File Sharing. When you re-open the Properties dialog for the Accounting folder, you will see that a Security tab has been added to the Accounting folder. Using the Security tab, you can implement advanced security settings at the Accounting folder.

**Step 2.** The default permissions for the Accounting folder are these:

- Administrators—Full Control (inherited from the NTFS drive)
- SYSTEM—Full Control (inherited from the NTFS drive)
- CREATOR OWNER—Full Control (inherited from the NTFS drive)
- Users—Read and Execute

**Step 3.** Select the Users account, and click Remove. An error message should appear, stating that you cannot remove the Users object because it is inheriting permissions. To remove the object, you must prevent it from inheriting permissions. Click OK.

**Step 4.** To remove the inherited permissions from the Users group, click the Advanced button on the Security tab of the object. At the Permissions tab, select the Users entry. Clear the Inherit From Parent The Permissions Entries That Apply To Child Objects check box. Click OK. Read the security message, and click Remove. All account entries that have inherited permissions are removed from the permission entries list.

**Step 5.** At the Security tab of the Properties dialog for the Accounting folder, click Add. Browse to the Administrators account in the list of user accounts, and add Administrators to the security list. Grant the Full Control permission to the Administrators group.

**Step 6.** At the Security tab of the Properties dialog for the Accounting folder, click Add. Browse to and add the Mike user account to the security list of user accounts. Grant the Full Control permission to the Mike account.

**Step 7.** At the Security tab of Properties dialog for the Accounting folder, click the Advanced button. At the Permissions tab in the Advanced Security Settings dialog, select the Administrators group. Click Edit, and verify that the permissions are applied to the Accounting folder and all its subfolders and files (Figure 9-2). Click OK.

**Step 8.** At the Permissions tab in the Advanced Security Settings dialog for the Accounting folder, ensure that the Mike account has the new setting of Full Control that applies to the Accounting folder and any subfolders. Click OK. Close all open windows.

Checking the
NTFS folder and
file permissions
for the user group
Administrators

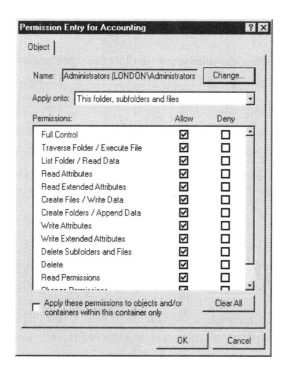

**Step 9.** Browse to the Computer Management administrative tool. At the Computer Management tool, check the Local Users | Users container for the Cheryl user account. Close all windows and log off the computer.

**Step 10.** Use Windows Explorer to browse to the Accounting folder while logged on as Cheryl. When you try to open the folder, you should be unable to do so, because you have granted access only to the Mike user account and the Administrators group. Log off the computer.

## Lab Solution 9.04

You should have arranged the permissions on Cathy's Management folder as described here.

**Step 1.** Create the **Managers** security group at the Computer Management console, and add the Mike user account to the group.

**Step 2.** The Management folder and the Private File text file should now exist on the NTFS-formatted drive.

**Step 3.**    In the My Documents folder, right-click the Management folder, and open the Properties dialog. Click the Sharing tab. By denying folder access to the Managers security group here, you prevent any Manager from seeing information in the Management folder over the network. By clearing all permissions for the Everyone group, you also deny access to any Manager who also belongs to the Everyone group.

**Step 4.**    Assigning the Managers group the Read, Read And Execute, and List Folder Contents permissions gives them access to the Private File text file within the Management folder when they log on locally. By clearing all permissions for the Everyone group, you preventing those permissions from overriding the Managers group permissions for users who are members of both groups. The Administrators group should already have the Full Control permission by default. Click OK. Log off the computer.

**Step 5.**    As Mike, you should be able to access the Private File text file through the Management folder. The Mike user account is a member of the Management group, and that group has been explicitly assigned the NTFS-security permissions Read, Read And Execute, and List Folder Contents when logging on locally.

**Step 6.**    As Mike, you should not be able to access the Private File text file through the Management share. The Mike user account is a member of the Managers group, and that group has been explicitly denied permissions to the Management folder. Log off the computer.

## Lab Solution 9.05

Your procedure to help Mike set up a virtual directory should resemble the one described here.

**Step 1.**    To open the IIS console, select Start | Programs | Administrative Tools | Internet Information Services. Figure 9-3 shows the Internet Information Services console with Default Web Site selected.

**Step 2.**    Right-click Default Web Site in the left pane of the console. Choose New | Virtual Directory. The Virtual Directory Creation wizard opens. Click Next. Giving the new virtual directory the friendly name **Mike's Web Site** will make it easy to recognize. Click Next.

**FIGURE 9-3**

Opening
the Internet
Information
Services console
and expanding
to the Default
Web Site

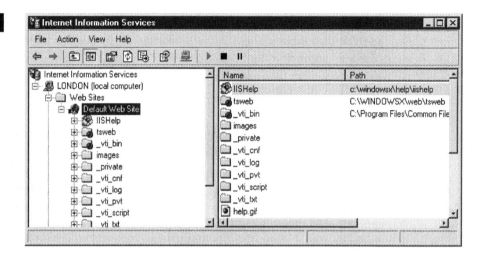

**Step 3.** Figure 9-4 shows the path to the directory that contains the web content. Click Next.

**Step 4.** Once you have verified the permissions (Figure 9-5), choose Execute. Click Next, and then click Finish. The new virtual directory should appear in the IIS console after you have successfully completed the wizard.

**FIGURE 9-4**

Specifying the path
to a virtual directory
that contains web
site content

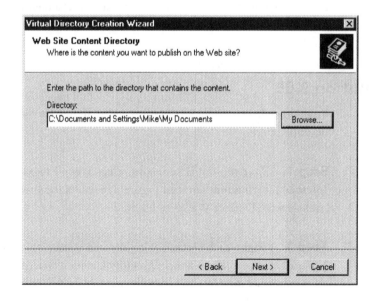

**FIGURE 9-5**

Setting access
permissions for
the new virtual
directory

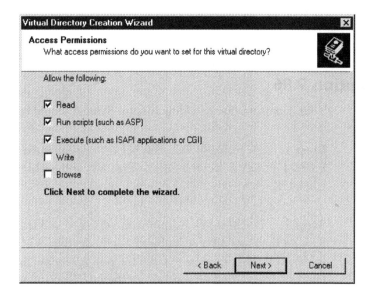

**Step 5.** To check the default authentication method, right-click Mike's Web
Site, and choose Properties. In the Properties dialog, select the Directory Security
tab. Click the Edit button. The Authentication Methods tab indicates that the
default authentication for the new virtual directory is Anonymous Access
(Figure 9-6). Anonymous access is configured by default so that users do not have

**FIGURE 9-6**

Checking
the default
authentication
method for a
new web folder

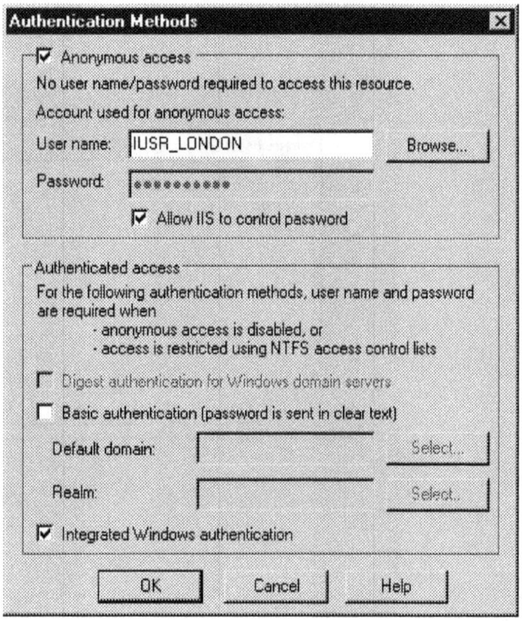

to provide a username and password, which is typical of web folder access. Close all open windows.

## Lab Solution 9.06

Your demonstration of offline files for Samuel should have gone something like this.

**Step 1.** To enable offline files, begin by opening the Control Panel. Double-click Folder Options. Select the Offline Files tab, and enable the Offline Files options. Click OK.

**Step 2.** Double-click Administrative Tools, and then Computer Management. Expand the Shared Folders object. Select the Shares object. Right-click the Data folder, and select Properties from the pop-up menu. Select the Share Permissions tab, and assign the Everyone group the Full Control permission:

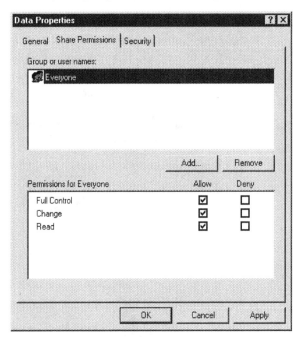

**Step 3.**    To verify the manual caching of documents, click the General tab, and select the Caching button. Once you have verified manual caching settings, click OK:

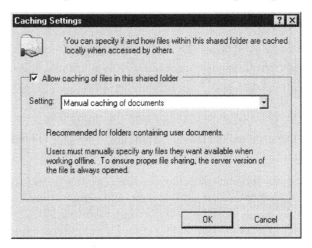

Close all open windows.

**Step 4.**    Use the Computer Management administrative tool to create the **John** user account on computer B.

**Step 5.**    Using the Run dialog box, browse to the shared folder called **Data** on computer A. Open the Data folder. Create the **Offline Test** text document.

**Step 6.** To open the Offline Test text document, double-click it. Make the change to the document, and save and close it. Right-click the modified document, and select Make Available Offline from the pop-up menu.

**Step 7.** When the Offline Files wizard opens, click Next to bypass the splash screen. Clear the Automatically Synchronize The Offline Files When I Log On And Log Off My Computer check box, if it is not already clear. Click Next.

Verify that Enable Reminders is selected. Select Create A Shortcut To The Offline Files Folder On My Desktop. Click Finish. Close any open windows. The shortcut to the Offline Files folder should now show on the Desktop.

**Step 8.** Double-click the shortcut to Offline Files. Double-click the Offline Test document. Close Offline Test, and close Offline Files. The process of opening and closing the Offline Test document automatically creates the offline file.

**Step 9.** To take computer B off the network, select Settings | Network Connections. At the Network Connections menu, right-click Local Area Connection, and click Disable. You can now work with a locally cached document on your Windows XP Professional computer.

**Step 10.** Double-click the shortcut to Offline Files. Double-click the Offline Test document. You should have been able to edit and save the locally cached version of Offline Test. Close the document.

**Step 11.** On the Taskbar, double-click the Offline Files Status icon. In the Offline File Status dialog, choose Work Online Without Synchronizing Changes. Click OK. Close the open window. On the Desktop, double-click the shortcut to Offline Files. Double-click the Offline Test document. The document should still have the changes that you applied, because you opened the locally cached version of the document.

**Step 12.** When you reconnect to the local area network, the locally cached version of Offline Test is synchronized with the shared version that was on the remote computer. If you were now to open the Offline Test document, you would be working with the version of the file from the network shared folder. Log off computer B. Log off computer A.

# ANSWERS TO LAB ANALYSIS TEST

1.  When share-level permissions and NTFS permissions are combined, the user receives the most restrictive permission.

2.  The combination of the specified NTFS and share-level permissions results in the most restrictive permission, which is Write in this case.

3.  If you copy a compressed file to a folder that is not compressed, the file will not retain its compression status. Instead, it inherits the uncompressed state of the destination folder. If the file were to be *moved* to a new location on the same NTFS partition, then the file would retain its compression status.

4.  Fast-user switching allows another user to log on and still see your application and open files. It is a way for several people to quickly use the same computer. Because offline files are tied to your username and require complete logon and logoff processes to close, they do not work with fast-user switching.

5.  IIS is provided with Windows XP Professional so that you can use Windows XP Professional as a web server, but IIS is not installed by default.

# ANSWERS TO KEY TERM QUIZ

1.  anonymous authentication

2.  Offline Files wizard

3.  manual caching of documents

4.  compression

5.  NTFS permissions

MICROSOFT CERTIFIED SYSTEMS ENGINEER

# 10

# Networking

## LAB EXERCISES

This chapter explores the ability of Windows XP Professional to function in a network environment, whether part of a Windows 2000 domain, a simple workgroup, or home network. Windows XP Professional is simple enough for the home user who wants to connect two PCs together and sophisticated enough to take advantage of advanced networking features.

In the following labs, you examine the TCP/IP protocol. You learn to configure TCP/IP with for dynamic, static, and automatic private IP addressing. You also create and configure dial-up connections, Virtual Private Network connections, and even Internet connection sharing.

**LAB EXERCISE 10.01**

# Configuring and Testing TCP/IP

**30 Minutes**

Steve wants to learn how to configure his IP address so that he knows when he is receiving an IP address from a Dynamic Host Configuration Protocol (DHCP) server, and when he is receiving an automatic IP address. He also wants to learn what other information needs to be configured when manually assigning an IP address. Finally, he wants to test his network connection and ensure that he can access resources.

## Learning Objectives

In this lab, you configure a network connection and test TCP/IP connectivity. At the end of the lab, you'll be able to

- Recognize your computer's IP address type.
- Obtain an automatic private IP address.
- Configure a static IP address with TCP/IP advanced settings.
- Test TCP/IP connectivity.

## Lab Materials and Setup

The materials you need for this lab are

■ Pencil and paper

■ Computer with Windows XP Professional installed

## Getting Down to Business

Here's how you'll help Steve with his questions about IP addresses.

**Step 1.** At your Windows XP Professional computer, open the Run dialog, and enter **cmd**. When the command prompt window opens, enter **ipconfig /all**.

From the results, record your IP address, subnet mask, and default gateway in the space provided. Are you receiving your IP address from a DHCP server?

_____

_____

Minimize the command prompt window.

**Step 2.** From the Desktop, open the Properties dialog for My Network Places, and then the Properties dialog for the Local Area Connection. Now open the Properties dialog the TCP/IP protocol. In the space provided, record whether your computer is configured to obtain an IP address automatically or whether one has been manually assigned. If necessary, change the setting to automatic address assignment.

_____

_____

**Step 3.** Open the Services administrative tool. Choose the DHCP Client service. Stop the service.

**Step 4.** Return to the command prompt window. At the prompt, enter **ipconfig /all**. What is the IP address of your Windows XP Professional computer now that the DHCP Client service has been stopped?

_____

_____

**Step 5.**   At the command prompt, type **ipconfig /renew**. Record the new address given to you, and define the type of address that you received. Attempt to browse the network. Were you able to do so? Close the command prompt window.

_____

_____

**Step 6.**   Return to the Network Connections window. Open the properties of the Local Area Connection. Open the TCP/IP protocol. Select Use The Following IP Address, and enter the information provided in Table 10-1. In a classroom setting, you can ask your instructor for the subnet number and computer number for your particular Windows XP Professional computer. If you are working at home, you can assign subnet and computer numbers of your choice.

lab
**Hint**    *If you are in a classroom that uses multiple subnets, ask your instructor for the IP address of the default gateway that should be used for your computer. If you are working at home, leave the default gateway blank.*

**Step 7.**   In the command prompt window, test your IP configuration by typing **ping 127.0.0.1**. Did you receive a reply?

_____

_____

**Step 8.**   If possible, obtain an IP address from another computer on the network and attempt to ping that computer. Were you able to reach the other computer on the network?

Open the Properties dialog for the TCP/IP protocol, and return the protocol to its original configuration, as recorded in step 1 of this lab. Ensure that you restart your DHCP Client service if necessary, and return your computer to its original state using the IP address and other data that you recorded in step 1.

| TABLE 10-1 | | |
|---|---|---|
| A Sample Static IP Configuration | **IP address** | 131.107.x.y. (x = subnet #, y = computer #) |
| | **Subnet mask** | 255.255.0.0 |
| | **Default gateway** | Leave blank |

## LAB EXERCISE 10.02

# Creating Incoming and Dial-Up Connections

**30 Minutes**

You have been asked to configure a Windows XP Professional computer to accept incoming connections from the Administrator and the Mike user accounts. The Administrator account should be able to have the computer call back at a specified number; the Mike user account should not be able to request a callback from the Windows XP Professional computer. On the same computer, you have been asked to create a dial-up outgoing connection for Mike's user account exclusively.

## Learning Objectives

In this lab, you implement an automated remote installation of Windows XP Professional for a medium-sized company. At the end of the lab, you'll be able to

■ Create an advanced connection.

■ Configure acceptance of incoming connections.

■ Configure user permissions.

## Lab Materials and Setup

The materials you need for this lab are

■ Pencil and paper

■ Local network computer with Windows XP Professional installed

■ Modem installed *or* Standard 56,000 modem software installed (from lab 5.01)

## Getting Down to Business

Configuring incoming and outgoing network connections is a standard piece of work for a Windows XP Professional. Here's how to set up the connectivity requested for this lab:

**Step 1.** Log on to the computer as Administrator. Open the properties for My Network Places. Choose to create a new network connection task.

**Step 2.**   Choose to create an advanced connection.

**Step 3.**   Choose to accept incoming connections, and choose your modem (or the Standard 56,000 modem) from the list of devices.

**Step 4.**   Disallow virtual private connections, and allow Administrator callers to set the callback number. Let the Mike user account also use this incoming connection (but without the ability to set the callback number).

**Step 5.**   At the Networking Software screen, ensure that all check boxes are enabled for incoming connections.

**Step 6.**   Using the Properties of the incoming connection, require all users to secure their passwords and data.

**Step 7.**   Begin creating another new network connection.

**Step 8.**   This time, you want to create a dial-up connection to the network at your workplace. Enter **Moran Solutions** as the company name at the Connection Name screen.

**Step 9.**   Type the number 555-3333 into the Phone Number field, and finish creating the connection. The Moran Solutions dial-up window appears. Enter username **Mike** with a password of **password**. Save the configuration for Mike only. Close the Moran Solutions dial-up window.

### LAB EXERCISE 10.03

# Creating a Virtual Private Network Connection with Internet Connection Sharing

**30 Minutes**

Steve uses a shared Windows XP Professional computer at the Kansas City sales office to connect to a remote-access server in the central Manhattan office. Steve wants to ensure that all users are able to connect to the remote-access server through a single connection on the computer. He also wants to implement advanced security settings on the connection, so that all data will be encrypted when sent across the network.

## Learning Objectives

In this lab, you configure a Virtual Private Network (VPN) connection for Steve and other users at McKinnon Industries who use a shared Windows XP Professional computer. At the end of the lab, you'll be able to

- Create a VPN connection.
- Configure advanced security settings.
- Configure Internet connection sharing (ICS).

## Lab Materials and Setup

For this lab exercise, you'll need

- Pencil and paper
- Computer with Windows XP Professional installed

## Getting Down to Business

Use this procedure the set up the necessary VPN connection:

**Step 1.**   To create the VPN connection, start the New Network Connection wizard.

**Step 2.**   Choose to connect to the network at work.

**Step 3.**   Choose to create a Virtual Private Network connection, and give the company name as **McKinnon Industries**. You should choose not to dial the Moran Solutions connection that was created in the previous lab.

**Step 4.**   At the VPN Server Selection screen, enter the IP address **196.182.3.45**, and finish the dial-up connection. When the Connection dialog box opens, enter the username **SSmith** with a password of **password**. Choose to save the password for all users of the computer. Open the connection properties.

lab
**Hint**

*For the purposes of this lab, you are using a simple password. However, in a live network environment, you must ensure that your passwords are complex.*

**Step 5.**    Open the Advanced Security Settings window for the new connection, and ensure that data encryption is set on. Deselect the Microsoft CHAP (MS-CHAP) check box. Select the For MS-CHAP Based Protocols, Automatically Use My Windows Logon Name And Password (And Domain If Any) check box. Click OK.

lab

**Hint**

*A VPN requires that the exact same setup be configured on both sides. Additionally, when troubleshooting, you should begin by choosing the lowest level of security available. Once the connection works, you can then start adding additional security features.*

**Step 6.**    Enable Internet connection sharing (Advanced tab of the connection properties), while not allowing other users to control or disable the connection.

# LAB ANALYSIS TEST

1.  If you wanted to check the route an IP packet took from the originating computer to the destination computer, what tool could you use?

    _____

    _____

2.  When you configure an incoming connection, will the protocols and services that you enable affect the outgoing connection as well?

    _____

    _____

3.  Can Internet connection sharing be used on a dial-up or LAN connection?

    _____

    _____

4.  What callback options are available on a Windows XP Professional dial-up connection?

    _____

    _____

5.  What is the defined automatic private IP addressing (APIPA) address range and default subnet mask for that address range?

    _____

    _____

# KEY TERM QUIZ

Use the following vocabulary terms to complete the sentences below. Not all of the terms will be used.

automatic private IP addressing (APIPA)

challenge handshake authentication protocol (CHAP)

dynamic host configuration protocol (DHCP)

extensible authentication protocol (EAP)

Internet connection sharing (ICS)

Layer 2 tunneling protocol (L2TP)

Microsoft CHAP (MS-CHAP)

Microsoft CHAP Version 2 (MS-CHAP v2)

nbtstat

netstat

nslookup

password authentication protocol (PAP)

pathping

point-to-point protocol (PPP)

point-to-point tunneling protocol (PPTP)

route

Shiva password authentication protocol (SPAP)

tracert

virtual private network (VPN)

1. The _____ , offered first in VPNs, provides mutual authentication and different encryption keys for sending and receiving.

2. The _____ supports tunnel authentication, data encryption with IP security (IPSec), and header compression.

3. The _____ uses clear-text passwords and provides low-level security.

4. _____ checks the status of NetBIOS over TCP/IP connections, and can give you information about the NetBIOS caches and the current sessions, and statistics.

5. _____ is used to look up IP address to DNS mappings in a DNS database.

# LAB WRAP-UP

You should now be familiar with configuring and testing TCP/IP connections. Additionally, you should be able to create and configure dial-up and VPN connections to access servers remotely in a network environment. You should also be familiar with the authentication and encryption protocols that are used with VPN connections, as well as with the TCP/IP utilities that are used to test TCP/IP connections.

# LAB SOLUTIONS FOR CHAPTER 10

In this section, you'll find solutions to the lab exercises, lab analysis test, and key term quiz.

## Lab Solution 10.01

Helping Steve to learn the details of IP addressing should have involved these steps.

**Step 1.** Answers will vary. However, if you are receiving an IP address from a DHCP server, DHCP Enabled will be set to **Yes**, and an IP address will be indicated for a DHCP server.

**Step 2.** Right-click My Network Places, and select Properties. Right-click your Local Area Connection, and select Properties. Select the TCP/IP protocol, and click Properties. In the TCP/IP Properties window that opens, does your computer obtain an IP address automatically or has one been manually assigned?

Answers will vary. If the TCP/IP Properties window indicates that the connection is already configured to obtain an IP address automatically, then no extra configuration is necessary. Otherwise, select the radio button labeled Obtain An IP Address Automatically. Click OK.

Minimize the Network Connections window.

**Step 3.** You can access the Services administrative tool from the Administrative tools menu or from the Computer Management console. Double-click DCHP Client to select it. At the General tab, click the Stop button to stop the service. The DHCP Client should show the status Stopped.

**Step 4.** Maximize the command prompt window. Once the DHCP Client service has been stopped, the network connection will indicate that no IP Address is available for the client. The IP address should be 0.0.0.0.

**Step 5.** Upon you renewal of the IP address, Windows XP Professional provides an automatic private IP address for your computer in the range 169.254.x.y. It uses that range because it is unable to contact a DHCP server to receive an IP address from the DHCP address pool. If other computers on the network have also received automatic private IP addresses, you should be able to connect to those computers and share resources. If other computers on the network have received automatic IP addresses from the DHCP server, you will be unable to communicate with those computers.

**Step 6.**   In the Network Connections window, right-click the Local Area Connection, and select Properties. At the General tab, double-click the TCP/IP protocol. Select Use The Following IP Address, and enter the information as instructed in the scenario. Figure 10-1 shows a sample static TCP/IP configuration. Individual computer IP configurations will vary slightly.
    Click OK. Minimize the Network Connections window.

**Step 7.**   Performing a loopback test on your network adapter card by pinging the local host should produce a reply .

**Step 8.**   You should be able to access other computers on your local network, provided they have also indicated an IP address that is local to your subnet.
    When you are done checking network access, maximize the Network Connections window, and right-click the Local Area Connection. Select Properties. Double-click the TCP/IP protocol, and return the configuration to its original state. Close all open windows.

**FIGURE 10-1**

Configuring
a computer
with a static
IP address

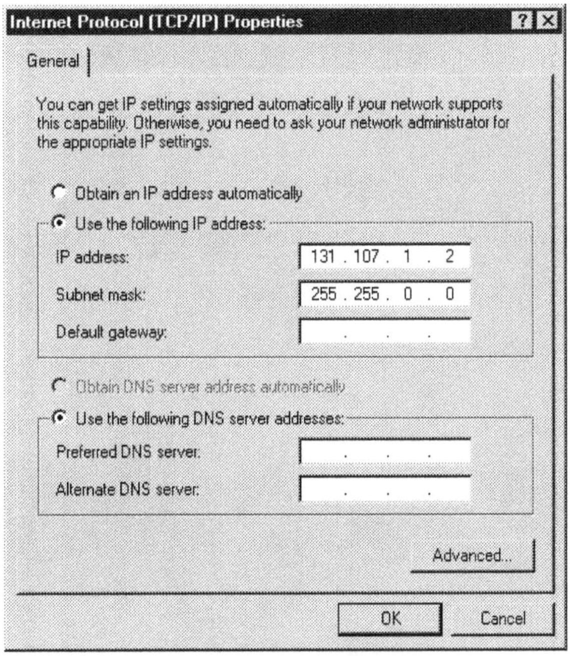

## Lab Solution 10.02

Your connectivity setup for the Windows XP Professional computer should resemble the one described here.

**Step 1.**   On the desktop, right-click My Network Places, and select Properties from the pop-up menu. Click Create A New Network Connection. The New Network Connection wizard starts. Click Next to move past the welcome screen.

**Step 2.**   At the Network Connection Type screen, select Set Up An Advanced Connection. Click Next.

**Step 3.**   At the Advanced Connection Options page, select Accept Incoming Connections. Click Next. Select the check box that corresponds to your modem (or the Standard 56,000 modem). (Figure 10-2 shows a typical choice.) Click Next.

**Step 4.**   At the Incoming Virtual Private Network Connection screen, select Do Not Allow Virtual Private Connections. Click Next.
    Select the check box for the Administrator account. Click the Properties button. Select the Callback tab. Select the radio button labeled Allow The Caller To Set The Callback Number. Click OK.

**FIGURE 10-2**

Choosing
a modem
to handle
an incoming
connection

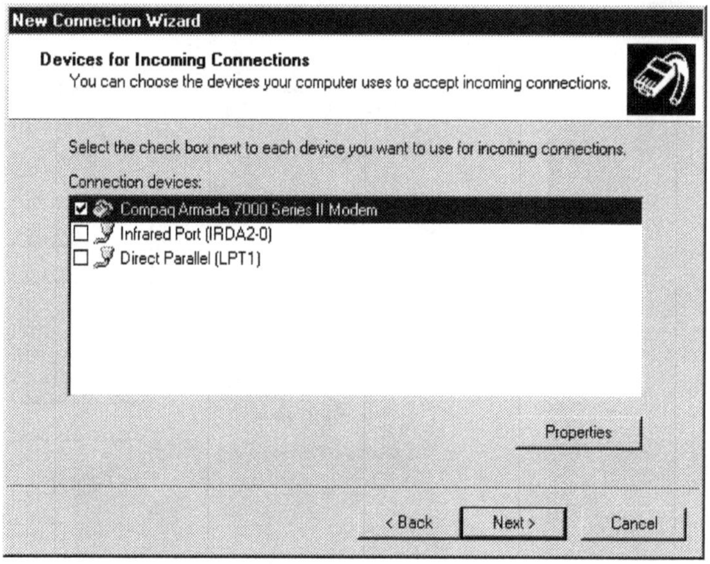

Giving the Mike
user account
permission
to use an
incoming
connection

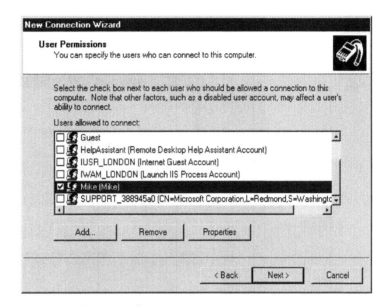

At the User permissions screen (Figure 10-3), select the check box for the Mike user account. Click Next.

**Step 5.**    Once you have made sure that all networking software is enabled for incoming connections, the connection should be created successfully. Click Next, and then Finish.

**Step 6.**    In the Network Connections window, right-click the newly created incoming connection object, and select Properties. Select the Users tab. Select the check box labeled Require All Users To Secure Their Passwords And Data (Figure 10-4). Click OK.

**Step 7.**    In the My Network Places window, click Create A New Network Connection. The New Network Connection wizard opens. Click Next to move past the welcome screen.

**Step 8.**    At the Network Connection Type screen, select Connect To The Network At My Workplace. Click Next.
At the Network Connection screen, select Dial-Up Connection. Click Next.

**FIGURE 10-4**

Requiring secure
data and passwords
for all users of the
connection

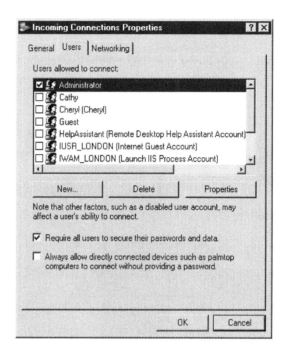

Enter **Moran Solutions** in the Company Name text box at the Connection Name
screen (Figure 10-5). Click Next.

**FIGURE 10-5**

Giving a name
to a connection

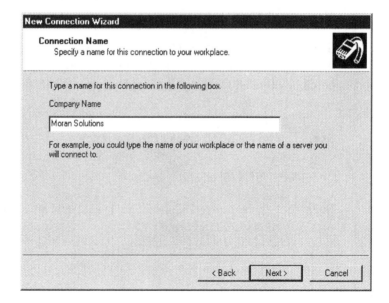

**FIGURE 10-6**

Viewing the details
of the newly
created connection

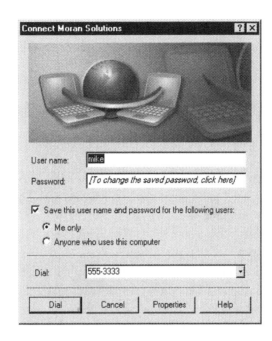

**Step 9.** After you type the phone number, click Next, and then Finish. The phone number 555-3333 on the remote server should show on the Phone Number To Dial tab, and the dial-up connection should have been created successfully (Figure 10-6). Mike's username and password should be entered and saved only for his user account.

## Lab Solution 10.03

The single connection that Steve wants should have been configured as described here.

**Step 1.** Right-click My Network Places, and select Properties from the pop-up menu. Click Create A New Network Connection. When the New Network Connection wizard opens, click Next to move past the welcome screen.

**Step 2.** At the Network Connection Type screen, select Connect To The Network At My Workplace. Click Next.

**Step 3.** At the Network Connection screen, select Virtual Private Network Connection. Click Next.

Enter **McKinnon Industries** at the Connection Name screen. Click Next.
At the Public Network screen, select Do Not Dial The Initial Connection.
Click Next.

**Step 4.**   After you enter the IP address of the computer to which you will connect, click Next, and then click Finish. Complete the Connection dialog box as described in the scenario. Click the Properties button.

**Step 5.**   At the Connection Properties dialog, click the Security tab. Select the Advanced radio button, and click Settings. The Advanced Security dialog should be configured as shown in Figure 10-7.

**Step 6.**   Click the Advanced tab. Enable the Internet Connection Sharing option. Clear the check box labeled Establish A Dial-Up Connection Whenever A Computer On My Network Attempts To Access The Internet. Clear the check box labeled Allow Other Network Users To Control Or Disable The Shared Internet Connection. Click OK.

**FIGURE 10-7**

Configuring
advanced security
for a VPN
connection

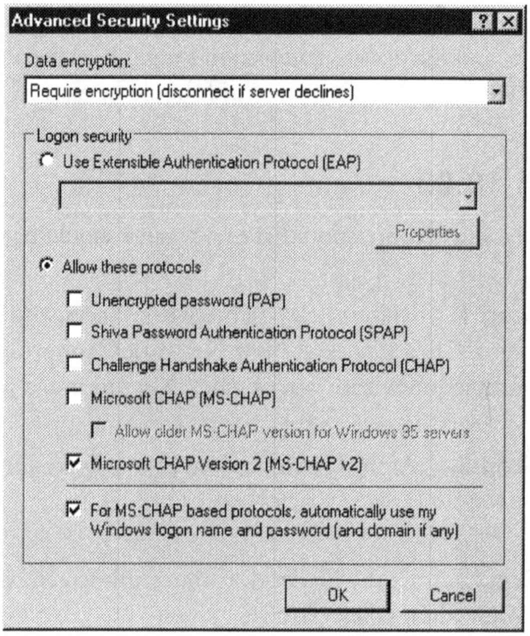

# ANSWERS TO LAB ANALYSIS TEST

1. Tracert is a simple utility that traces the route from one host to another. If you were using the ping utility to test connections, the Pathping tool would be useful, because you can ping an address or DNS name and see the actual route of the ping.

2. When you configure an incoming connection protocol or service, the configuration affects only that incoming connection. Outgoing connections are completely independent and require their own configuration.

3. ICS can be used on a dial-up, LAN, VPN, point-to-point over Ethernet (PPPoE), or broadband Internet connection. The host computer should have a connection to the Internet and a network adapter card for local network connectivity. Client computers need have only a network adapter card to be able to connect to the ICS host.

4. Windows XP Professional supports callback options on a dial-up connection. You can choose to disable callback, to enable callback to a number defined by the caller, or to enable callback to a predefined number.

5. When APIPA is used, an IP address from the address range 169.254.0.0 to 169.254.255.255 is used, along with a subnet mask of 255.255.0.0.

# ANSWERS TO KEY TERM QUIZ

1. Microsoft CHAP Version 2 (MS-CHAP v2)

2. Layer 2 tunneling protocol (L2TP)

3. password authentication protocol (PAP)

4. nbtstat

5. nslookup

MICROSOFT CERTIFIED SYSTEMS ENGINEER

# 11

# Internet and Remote Networking

W indows XP Professional provides the Internet Explorer web browser for Internet and intranet usage. You can customize the security and privacy settings of Internet Explorer to suit the security requirements of your company or to protect your home computer from security risks.

Windows XP Professional also offers Remote Assistance and Remote Desktop features. Remote Assistance allows you to access another person's Windows XP computer remotely—over the Internet or a wide-area network (WAN), for example—so that you can troubleshoot and solve problems. Remote Desktop enables you to open a terminal session with a Windows XP Professional system so that you can use the computer remotely. This chapter examines each of those remote features.

Windows XP Professional also includes a personal firewall in the Internet Connection Firewall (ICF) and the Internet Information Services (IIS) component managed through the Internet Services Manager console. You'll also configure each of those components to suit your remote networking needs.

**LAB EXERCISE 11.01**

# Configuring Internet Explorer Security and Privacy Settings

**20 Minutes**

You have been hired by Clark & Associates to configure browsing security and privacy settings on 500 Windows XP Professional client computers. The management at Clark & Associates wants you to configure security settings both for the company's local intranet and for the Internet. They have given you a list of security and privacy requirements that must be implemented on all client computers. They have asked you to configure a single Windows XP Professional computer in a test environment before recommending a 500-unit rollout solution.

## Learning Objectives

In this lab, you examine Internet Explorer security and privacy settings. At the end of the lab, you'll be able to

- Configure and identify Internet security settings.
- Configure and identify local intranet security settings.
- Configure and manage privacy settings.

## Lab Materials and Setup

The materials you need for this lab are

- Pencil and paper
- Windows XP Professional computer with Internet Explorer web browser
- Connection to the Internet

## Getting Down to Business

In this lab, you apply the knowledge that you acquired in the *MCSE Windows XP Professional Study Guide* by Curt Simmons (McGraw-Hill/Osborne, 2002) for configuring Internet Explorer security and privacy settings.

**Step 1.** Log on to the Windows XP Professional computer as Administrator. Starting from the Control Panel, configure each of the Web content zones to meet the requirements of Clark & Associates as shown here:

| Internet | Prompt to run ActiveX controls and plug-ins |
|---|---|
| Local intranet | Do not include all sites that bypass the proxy server<br>Add **www.dailywonklists.com** to the zone |
| Trusted sites | Medium-low custom settings level |
| Restricted sites | Add **www.yahoo.com** to the zone |

**Step 2.** Configure the privacy setting for Clark & Associates to medium-high, and arrange to enable prompting for third-party cookies.

**Step 3.** Add the **http://www.dailywonklists.com** web site to the list of sites that are always allowed to use cookies regardless of the privacy policy. Save all the settings, and close the Internet Options window. Close the Control Panel window.

**Step 4.** What is the difference between first-party and third-party cookies? In the space provided, briefly define each type of cookie.

_____

_____

**Step 5.** Remove from Internet Options all security and privacy settings that you configured during this lab.

---

**LAB EXERCISE 11.02**

# Configuring and Using Remote Desktop

**30 Minutes**

Cathy would like to be able to run an application from her home computer (computer A) that she normally runs on her office Windows XP Professional computer (computer B). She has asked you to configure her office computer to allow her to connect to it remotely and run an application. She has also specified that she would like to view display settings identical to those used on her office computer when she connects remotely. You have discovered that Cathy is not using Internet Connection Firewall (ICF) or any other type of firewall on either her computer or the company network.

## Learning Objectives

In this lab, you configure and use remote desktop settings. At the end of the lab, you'll be able to

- Configure a Windows XP Professional computer for Remote Desktop.
- Connect to a computer running Remote Desktop.
- Configure Remote Desktop Connection display settings.

## Lab Materials and Setup

The materials you need for this lab are computer A and computer B, Windows XP Professional computers installed on the local network.

lab
Hint

*If you do not have access to two computers, you should focus on the requirements for using Remote Desktop during this lab.*

## Getting Down to Business

The following steps guide you through configuring and using Remote Desktop. You will have to apply the knowledge that you acquired in the *MCSE Windows XP Professional Study Guide* by Curt Simmons (McGraw-Hill/Osborne, 2002).

**Step 1.**   Log on to computer B as Administrator. Open the Properties for the computer, and arrange for all users to connect remotely to the computer. If a message appears, read the message, and click OK.

lab
Hint

*A message window may appear stating that accounts used for remote connections must have passwords and that correct ports must be opened on a firewall to enable remote connections.*

**Step 2.**   While still logged on to computer B, add the Cathy account from computer A to the list of available remote users.

lab
Hint

*The Cathy account was created on computer A in lab 9.02. If the account does not currently exist, you must create it on computer A and be able to access it from computer B.*

Log off computer B.

**Step 3.**   Log on to computer A as Cathy (password 2002JKL). Open the Remote Desktop Connection console.

**Step 4.**   At the General tab of the Remote Desktop Connection dialog, ensure that the names of computer B and the Cathy account appear for the connection information. Enter **2002JKL** as the password.

**Step 5.**   Select the Display tab and configure the remote desktop size to 800×600 pixels and the colors to True Color (24-bit). Ensure that the connection bar will be displayed in full mode. Click Connect.

**Step 6.**   When the Remote Desktop Connection starts, a taskbar for computer B will appear at the top of the screen. Verify that you can start an application on computer B from the Remote Desktop Connection window. Close the application.

**Step 7.**   Log off the remote desktop connection when prompted. Log off computer A.

**LAB EXERCISE 11.03**

**30 Minutes**

# Examining Remote Assistance

Dean has asked you to explain the Remote Assistance feature provided with Windows XP Professional. He is interested in using the Remote Assistance feature on his large company network. That way, he can provide support to his users from his desk rather than having to purchase additional support software or to physically visit each user's computer. He has asked you to define the basic features and give examples of what is required by Administrators and users on the network to be able to use Remote Assistance.

## Learning Objectives

In this lab, you configure and manage Remote Assistance settings. At the end of the lab, you'll be able to

- Define the benefits of Remote Assistance.
- Request help using Remote Assistance.
- Permit remote control of your Windows XP Professional computer.
- Offer help using Remote Assistance.

## Lab Materials and Setup

The materials you need for this lab are

■ Pencil and paper

■ Windows XP Professional computer

## Getting Down to Business

The following steps guide you through configuring and managing Remote Assistance. You will have to apply the knowledge that you acquired in the *MCSE Windows XP Professional Study Guide* by Curt Simmons (McGraw-Hill/Osborne, 2002).

**Step 1.** In the space provided, define the benefits provided by the Remote Assistance feature of Windows XP Professional.

_____

_____

**Step 2.** List the requirements for your Windows XP Professional computer to be able to implement Remote Assistance on your network.

_____

_____

**Step 3.** What steps must you take to invite someone to remotely control your Windows XP Professional computer?

_____

_____

**Step 4.** What information is required by an Administrator to offer remote assistance to a user's computer on a local network?

_____

_____

**Step 5.** What type of information can be configured in a Remote Assistance e-mail invitation?

_____

_____

**LAB EXERCISE 11.04**

# Configuring Internet Connection Firewall

15 Minutes

Mike wants to prevent access to his Windows XP Professional computer from the Internet. He wants to have the firewall allow FTP, HTTP, POP3, and SMTP traffic. He also wants to log successful connections to his computer and to prevent incoming data transmissions that his computer cannot keep up with owing to their fast rates of transmission.

## Learning Objectives

In the following lab, you configure an Internet Connection Firewall on a Windows XP Professional computer. At the end of the lab, you'll be able to

- ▦ Protect a Windows XP Professional computer with Internet Connection Firewall.
- ▦ Configure services to allow Internet access.
- ▦ Establish security logging on the firewall.
- ▦ Allow outgoing Internet Control Message Protocol (ICMP) messages on the firewall.

## Lab Materials and Setup

For this lab exercise, you'll need a computer with Windows XP Professional installed.

## Getting Down to Business

These steps guide you in configuring an Internet Connection Firewall for a Windows XP Professional computer. You will have to apply the knowledge that you acquired in the *MCSE Windows XP Professional Study Guide* by Curt Simmons (McGraw-Hill/Osborne, 2002).

**Step 1.**   At the Windows XP Professional computer, open the Properties for your LAN connection. Select the Advanced tab.

**Step 2.**   Enable the Internet Connection Firewall (ICF). Click Settings.

**Step 3.**   Allow users on the Internet to access the POP3, SMTP, FTP, and HTTP services running on your local network.

**Step 4.**   Select the option to log successful connections to the default log name and location.

**Step 5.**   Select the option to drop data that has a rate of transmission too fast for the Windows XP Professional computer to process. Save all settings and close the ICF properties.

# LAB ANALYSIS TEST

1. After you add a particular web site to the restricted zone in Internet Explorer, does the site become inaccessible to users?

   _____

   _____

2. During Remote Assistance, how can a user always retains control of the connection and terminate it at any time?

   _____

   _____

3. What must be configured in Internet Connection Firewall to allow Remote Desktop connections?

   _____

   _____

4. What is the function of a Remote Desktop Web Connection?

   _____

   _____

5. What operating systems support Remote Desktop connections?

   _____

   _____

# KEY TERM QUIZ

Use the following vocabulary terms to complete the sentences below. Not all of the terms will be used.

first-party cookie

Internet Connection Firewall (ICF)

Internet Control Message Protocol (ICMP)

Medium security

Medium-Low security

persistent cookie

Remote Assistance

Remote Desktop

restricted sites

Secure Sockets Layer (SSL)

third-party cookie

trusted sites

1. A _____ is stored as a file on your computer and can be read by the web site that created it whenever you visit that site.

2. _____ is a TCP/IP protocol that computers can use to exchange network condition information and transmission failure information.

3. _____ on the IE web browser prevents unsigned ActiveX controls from being downloaded. It is also an appropriate setting for sites on your local intranet.

4. _____ inspects TCP/IP traffic at the packet level, and then determines which IP packets are allowed onto your network and which are not.

5. With _____ , a user can access another user's computer over a WAN, such as the Internet, and actually troubleshoot the other user's computer.

# LAB WRAP-UP

You should now be familiar with the Internet and intranet security and privacy features that Windows XP Professional offers through the Internet Explorer web browser. You should know how to establish and configure a Remote Desktop Connection and be familiar the Remote Assistance feature of Windows XP Professional. Finally, you should have successfully configured and implemented the Internet Connection Firewall feature on your personal computer.

# LAB SOLUTIONS FOR CHAPTER 11

In this section, you'll find solutions to the lab exercises, lab analysis test, and key term quiz.

## Lab Solution 11.01

The 500-unit rollout solution for Clark & Associates should look something like this.

**Step 1.** At the Control Panel, double-click Internet Options. Select the Security tab. Each Web security zone should be configured in accordance with the settings outlined in the scenario. The Internet zone should prompt a user before running ActiveX controls and plug-ins. The local intranet should not include sites that bypass the proxy server, and the DailyWonkLists.com web site should be added to the zone. The trusted sites should have their default security increased from Low to Medium-Low, and the restricted sites should include the Yahoo.com web site in its zone.

**Step 2.** Select the Privacy tab. You can configure the privacy setting for Clark & Associates here. In terms of privacy, the Clark & Associates privacy setting should increase from Medium to Medium-High to block first-party cookies that use personally identifiable information without implicit consent. Click the Advanced button. Select the Override Automatic Cookie Handling check box. Overriding the privacy setting enables prompting for third-party cookies. Click OK.

**Step 3.** From the Privacy tab, click the Edit button. Add the **http://www.dailywonklists.com** web site as directed. Click OK to save settings, and close the windows as directed.

**Step 4.** A first-party cookie originates or is sent from the web site that you are viewing. In other words, it comes from contact between your browser and the web site. A third-party cookie originates from a web site that you are not viewing. Typically, the cookie is generated because you click on some content on the first-party site, such as an advertisement.

**Step 5.** All configured security and privacy settings on the Internet Options object should be removed.

## Lab Solution 11.02

Here's how to configure remote connection for Cathy.

**Step 1.** Right-click My Computer on the Desktop, and click Properties. In the My Computer Properties dialog, select the Remote tab. Allow all users to connect remotely to the computer. The Cathy user account used for remote access should have a password, as defined in an earlier lab.

**Step 2.** Click the Select Remote Users button. At the Remote Desktop Users window, click Add. Give the remote user Cathy from computer A access to computer B. Save all settings, and close all windows.

**Step 3.** To open the Remote Desktop Connection console, select Start | Programs | Accessories | Communications | Remote Desktop Connection.

**Step 4.** The remote connection information for computer B, with the Cathy user account and password (2002JKL) should appear in the connection fields on the General tab of the Remote Desktop Connection window.

**Step 5.** The Display tab should indicate the 800×600 remote desktop size and show that True Color (24-bit) is being used. The connection bar should also be selected to display in full mode. The Connect button should initiate the connection.

**Step 6.** You should be able to successfully start an application from the Remote Desktop Connection window.

**Step 7.** To log off the remote desktop connection, click Start | Log Off at the Remote Desktop Connection window when prompted.

## Lab Solution 11.03

You gladly tell Dean how to use Remote Assistance to make his job of supporting his users easier.

**Step 1.** Remote Assistance provides a user at another computer with the ability to view your computer screen and to chat online with you in real time about what you both see. Remote Assistance also provides the other user, with your permission, the ability to use your keyboard or mouse to work with you on your computer.

**Step 2.** To be able to run Remote Assistance, you and your remote partner must both be running either Windows Messenger or a MAPI-compliant e-mail client such as Microsoft Outlook Express or Outlook. You must also both be connected to the Internet while running Remote Assistance. Any firewalls on the network must permit communication between the two computers. Remote Assistance works only with Windows XP computers. In other words, you can't use Remote Assistance from your XP computer and assist someone using a Windows Me computer unless that person installs the Remote Assistance Client software found on the Windows XP Professional CD.

**Step 3.** You use the Help and Support Center to send a remote assistance invitation through an e-mail client or Windows Messenger. To begin, the Windows XP Professional (or Client) computer must be configured to allow Remote Assistance invitations to be sent. You can do that by selecting the Remote Assistance check box on the Remote tab of the System Properties dialog. The other user can then configure their computer to allow remote control. The process involves selecting the Advanced button on the Remote tab of the System Properties dialog, and then specifying Allow This Computer To Be Controlled Remotely.

**Step 4.** An Administrator can offer help to a local area network user if the Administrator knows the computer name or IP address of the computer to which they want to connect. The Administrator can enter that information in the Help and Support Center console and attempt to connect to the remote computer.

**Step 5.** In a Remote Assistance e-mail invitation from the Help and Support Center, you can configure the invitation to expire after a defined number of minutes, hours, or days. You can also require the recipient of the invitation to provide a password when attempting to connect to your computer remotely.

## Lab Solution 11.04

Here's how to configure a firewall solution for Mike.

**Step 1.** Right-click My Network Places, and select Properties. View the Properties for the LAN connection, and select the Advanced tab in that dialog.

**Step 2.** Select the check box that enables the Internet Connection Firewall. The Settings button opens the available configuration options on the ICF.

**Step 3.** To allow users from the Internet to access the specified services on your Windows XP Professional computer, you need to select all of them at the Services tab of the ICF.

**Step 4.** You can find the option to log successful connections on the Security logging tab on the ICF. Use the default log name and location for the security log.

**Step 5.** To drop any data that has a rate of transmission too fast for the Windows XP Professional computer, select the Allow Outgoing Source Quench option on the ICMP tab in the ICF Properties dialog. Click OK to save all settings. Close the ICF object.

# ANSWERS TO LAB ANALYSIS TEST

1. Sites added to the Restricted Sites zone are not forbidden or inaccessible, they are simply configured with the High security setting. High security prevents the user from downloading unsigned ActiveX controls or other programs that may be unsafe.

2. Although an Administrator can access the user's computer and make configuration changes via the remote connection, the user always retains control of the connection. The connection can be forcefully terminated at any time by clicking Stop in Windows Messenger or pressing ESC on the keyboard.

3. By default, the Internet Connection Firewall does not allow Remote Desktop connections. If ICF is in use, you must enable Remote Desktop on the firewall for the remote connection to work.

4. Remote Desktop Web Connection is a web application consisting of an ActiveX control with sample ASP pages. It is deployed on a web server. Once the Remote Desktop Web Connection is deployed, users on the network can create a remote desktop connection to another computer through Internet Explorer. With this feature, users of other operating systems can generate remote desktop connections without the Remote Desktop software being installed. Also, operating systems not supported by the Remote Desktop software can use the web connection for cross-platform capability.

5. To use Remote Desktop, you need two Windows XP computers. However, you can also connect a Windows XP computer to a Windows 9*x*, 2000, NT, or Me computer by installing the Remote Desktop Client on those systems. Remote Desktop Client is available on the Windows XP Professional installation CD.

# ANSWERS TO KEY TERM QUIZ

1. persistent cookie

2. Internet Control Message Protocol (ICMP)

3. Medium-Low security

4. Internet Connection Firewall (ICF)

5. Remote Assistance

MICROSOFT CERTIFIED SYSTEMS ENGINEER

# 12

# Configuring, Managing, and Troubleshooting Security

## LAB EXERCISES

W indows XP Professional provides security features that enable users to keep data safe, and administrators to control how users and groups function on the system. In a domain environment, you will most likely configure security settings from the server level through group policies and related tools. However, you should also know how to manage Windows XP Professional at the local level, including user and group security settings, security templates through local group policies, and the Encrypting File System (EFS).

This chapter examines the various security templates that you can apply to a Windows XP Professional computer. You will configure a local security policy, implement the Encrypting File System (EFS), and manage local user and group accounts.

## LAB EXERCISE 12.01

# Working with the Encrypting File System

**60 Minutes**

A user named Mike is no longer with the company, but has left an encrypted folder and file on his office computer. Other users need access to the encrypted file. You determine that you will have to create and implement a recovery agent certificate to obtain access to the encrypted file.

## Learning Objectives

In this lab, you work with the Encrypting File System to encrypt and decrypt a user's files. At the end of the lab, you'll be able to

- Configure a recovery agent for the local computer.
- Export a recovery agent certificate.
- Encrypt a user folder with EFS.
- Test encryption attributes.
- Import a recovery agent certificate.
- Recover an encrypted file.

## Lab Materials and Setup

The materials you need for this lab are

- Pencil and paper
- Windows XP Professional computer
- Blank formatted floppy disk

## Getting Down to Business

In the following lab, you have to apply the knowledge you acquired in the *MCSE Windows XP Professional Study Guide* by Curt Simmons (McGraw-Hill/Osborne, 2002) for encrypting and decrypting files.

**Step 1.**   Log on to the computer as Administrator, and open the Microsoft Management Console (MMC). Prepare to add a snap-in. Choose to add the Certificates snap-in for the local user account.

**Step 2.**   In the MMC, expand Certificates until you can see the Administrator certificate. Select it. Choose to export the digital certificate together with your private key. Disable the strong protection option and assign a password of **1357cert**. Name the certificate **recovery.pfx**, and save it to your floppy disk. Close and save the console as **Certificates** in the Administrative Tools folder.

**Step 3.**   At the Windows XP Professional computer, log on using the Mike user account with a blank password. Create a folder called **Private** on the NTFS-formatted drive. Create a text document called **Private File** inside the folder. Open the file, and type the text **This file is private.** Save and close the file.

**Step 4.**   Open the Properties of the Private folder, and choose to encrypt all subfolders and files within the folder. Log off the computer.

**Step 5.**   Log on to the computer as Administrator. Open Windows Explorer and attempt to access Private File in the Private folder on the NTFS-formatted drive. Were you able to access the file? Minimize Windows Explorer.

_____

_____

**Step 6.** Open the Certificates console, and expand to see the Personal certificates. Choose to Import the certificate that you saved on the floppy disk. Ensure that you choose to view Personal Information Exchange (.pfx) files, so that you can see the certificate that you saved on the disk.

**Step 7.** Enter the password **1357cert** that you applied to the certificate upon export. Import the certificate to the personal certificate store. Maximize Windows Explorer and attempt to access the Private File text file. Were you able to read the contents of the file?

_____

_____

**Step 8.** Open the Properties dialog for the Private folder. Switch off encryption of the folder. Close all open windows, and log off the computer.

**LAB EXERCISE 12.02**

# Creating and Managing Local User and Group Accounts

**15 Minutes**

You are an administrator for a large research company. You have been assigned the task of creating several new local user and group accounts. All new user accounts must be assigned to an appropriate new group account. Password settings must be assigned to each user account.

## Learning Objectives

In this lab, you work with the local user and group accounts of Windows XP Professional. At the end of the lab, you'll be able to

- Create and manage local user accounts.
- Create local group accounts.
- Add users to built-in local groups.

## Lab Materials and Setup

The materials you need for this lab are

- Pencil and paper
- Windows XP Professional computer

## Getting Down to Business

The following steps guide you through creating and managing local user and group accounts. You will have to apply the knowledge you acquired in the *MCSE Windows XP Professional Study Guide* by Curt Simmons (McGraw-Hill/Osborne, 2002) to complete the lab.

**Step 1.** At the Windows XP Professional computer, log on as Administrator. Open the Computer Management administrative tool, and browse to the Local User and Group objects.

**Step 2.** Create local user and group accounts from this information:

| | | |
|---|---|---|
| **Dean** | User account | Password: 549HgkP<br>Password never expires |
| **George** | User account | Password: sl30r8f<br>User cannot change password |
| **Ali** | User account | Password: password<br>User must change password at next logon |
| **Keith** | User account | Password: f294ksx<br>User cannot change password |
| **Supervisors** | Group account | Members: Dean, George |
| **Staff** | Group account | Members: Ali, Keith |
| **Power Users** | Built-in group account | Members: Dean, George |

**Step 3.** Ensure that you can log on to the Windows XP Professional computer with each of the user accounts that you have created, and that the password settings are applied on each account.

**Step 4.** Ensure that the George user account has the ability to create user accounts as a member of the Power Users group. Close all windows and log off the computer.

**LAB EXERCISE 12.03**

# Configuring a Local Security Policy

**30 Minutes**

Your boss has asked you to create and test a local security policy on the company's shared Windows XP Professional computer. He has asked you to implement account policy settings that would combine several password and lockout settings. He has also asked you to configure an audit policy to track user logons and object access.

## Learning Objectives

In this lab, you create an account policy that is applied to all users on the local Windows XP Professional computer. At the end of the lab, you'll be able to:

- Configure a local security policy.
- Test the effects of password policy settings.
- Test the effects of account lockout policy settings.
- Test the effects of audit policy settings.

## Lab Materials and Setup

For this lab exercise, you'll need

- Pencil and paper
- Windows XP Professional computer

## Getting Down to Business

The following steps guide you through the process of configuring a local security policy. You will have to apply the knowledge that you acquired in the *MCSE Windows XP Professional Study Guide* by Curt Simmons (McGraw-Hill/Osborne, 2002) to complete the lab.

**Step 1.** Log on to the computer as Administrator. Open the MMC, and add the Group Policy snap-in to the console for the local computer.

**Step 2.** At the console, expand Local Computer Policy until you reach Password Policy. Configure the minimum password length to seven characters. Save the console as Policies in the Administrative Tools folder. Minimize the console.

**Step 3.** Open the Computer Management console and attempt to create a user named **Tony** with a password of **1234**. Were you able to create the user with that password? Minimize the Computer Management console.

_____

_____

**Step 4.** At the Policies console, select the Account Lockout Policy and configure the Account Lockout Threshold to three invalid logon attempts. What other settings does Windows XP Professional change as a result of your Account Lockout Threshold configuration? Click OK to accept the default suggested settings. Close all open windows.

_____

_____

**Step 5.** Log off the computer, and attempt to log back on at least three times using the Cathy account with an incorrect password.

lab
ⓗint
*The correct password for the Cathy user account is 2002JKL.* **You should have created the Cathy account in lab 9.02.**

Were you locked out of the Windows XP Professional computer, based on the account lockout policy that you configured while logged on as Administrator?

_____

_____

**Step 6.** Log on to the computer as Administrator. Open the Policies console, and expand Local Computer Policy until you reach the Audit Policy.

**Step 7.** Choose to audit successful and failed account logon events and failed object access. Save your settings, and close the console. Log off the computer.

**Step 8.** Log on to the computer as Dean with the password of 549HgkP. Attempt to access the Accounting folder on the NFTS-formatted drive. Log off the computer.

lab
ⓗint
*The Accounting folder was created in lab 9.01.*

**Step 9.**   Log on to the computer as Administrator. Open the Event Viewer from the Administrative tools menu. Select the Security log. What types of events are listed in the security log?

_____

_____

Close all open windows and log off the computer.

**LAB EXERCISE 12.04**

# Implementing Security Templates

**30 Minutes**

Your boss has asked you to compare the current security settings on your Windows XP Professional computer with the settings specified in the Highly Secure Workstation (hisecws) security template. He would then like you to apply the settings of the security template and verify that the settings changes have taken effect.

## Learning Objectives

In this lab, you create an account policy that will be applied to all users on the local Windows XP Professional computer. At the end of the lab, you'll be able to

- Examine Windows XP Professional security templates.
- Analyze computer security settings.
- Implement a security template.
- View the effects of implementing a policy using a security template.

## Lab Materials and Setup

For this lab exercise, you'll need

- Pencil and paper
- Windows XP Professional computer

## Getting Down to Business

The following steps guide you through implementing security templates. You will have to apply the knowledge that you acquired in the *MCSE Windows XP Professional Study Guide* by Curt Simmons (McGraw-Hill/Osborne, 2002) to complete the lab.

**Step 1.**  Log on to the computer as Administrator. Open the Policies console. Add the Security Configuration and Analysis snap-in to the console.

**Step 2.**  Right-click the Security Configuration and Analysis object, and then click Open Database. Type **Windows XP Database** into the File Name field. Click Open. List and describe the security templates that appear.

_____

_____

**Step 3.**  Select the hisecws template, and compare it to the current security state on the computer. Accept the default error log file name and path.

**Step 4.**  Expand Security Configuration and Analysis, and observe the results of the analysis. Review the settings for each object, and compare the database settings with the current computer settings.

**Step 5.**  Apply the hisecws template to the computer configuration.

**Step 6.**  Reanalyze the computer. Review the settings for each object, and compare the settings database with the updated computer settings. How have the settings changed?

_____

_____

**Step 7.**  To remove the security template that you applied, import the Setup security template from the Security Configuration and Analysis menu. Save and close the Policies console. Log off the computer.

## LAB ANALYSIS TEST

1. Can the Encryption File System (EFS) be configured on a drive that is not formatted with the NTFS file system?

_____

_____

2. Can local users and groups be configured on a Windows XP Professional computer in a Windows 2000 Active Directory domain?

_____

_____

3. After you add a user account to a built-in group, how can you determine the permissions that the user account will inherit based on the group membership?

_____

_____

4. Where can you view the default security templates offered by Windows XP Professional?

_____

_____

5. What characters are not valid in a user account name?

_____

_____

# KEY TERM QUIZ

Use the following vocabulary terms to complete the sentences below. Not all of the terms will be used.

Account policy

Audit policy

backup operators

Cipher command-line tool

Encrypting File System (EFS)

Group policy

Hisec*.inf template

network configuration

Power Users

private key

recovery agent

Rootsec template

Securedc template

User Rights policy

1. The _____ should be applied to domain controllers. It defines the security settings that are least likely to affect application compatibility.

2. A(n) _____ enables you to see what users are doing and accessing. The information is stored in the Security Log in Event Viewer.

3. User accounts that are members of the _____ group have the most administrative rights (with certain restrictions), including running legacy applications.

4. The _____ can be used with various switches to encrypt and decrypt Windows XP Professional data.

5. A(n) _____ can be assigned so that data can be recovered in the event that a user's private key is lost or corrupted, or that the user is no longer present on the network.

# LAB WRAP-UP

You have now examined the Encrypting File System (EFS) and how you can encrypt and decrypt files, with and without a private key. You should be familiar with the managing local user and group accounts and the default permissions of the built-in user and group accounts. You have also learned how to implement security policies and templates on a Windows XP Professional computer.

# LAB SOLUTIONS FOR CHAPTER 12

In this section, you'll find solutions to the lab exercises, lab analysis test, and key term quiz.

## Lab Solution 12.01

Your solution for recovering Mike's files for access by other users should proceed as described here.

**Step 1.** Click Start, and then Run. Into the Run box, type **mmc**, and click OK. On the File menu of the Microsoft Management Console, click Add/Remove Snap-in. In the Add/Remove Snap-in dialog, click Add. Add the Certificates snap-in as specified. Click Finish. Click Close. Click OK. The Certificates snap-in should now appear in the Microsoft Management Console.

**Step 2.** At the MMC, expand Certificates | Current User | Personal | Certificates. Select the Administrator certificate that you see there. Right-click the certificate, and choose All Tasks | Export from the pop-up menu. Complete the Export Certificate wizard as directed in the scenario. Save the certificate **recovery.pfx** as directed in the scenario. Close and save the console as Certificates to the Administrative Tools folder. The Administrator certificate and private key (recovery.pfx) should have been exported (with a password) from the Certificates console to a blank formatted floppy disk.

**Step 3.** Make sure that you are logged in as Mike. Create a folder named **Private** from within Windows Explorer. Create, edit, and save the text document **Private File** using any convenient application. The Private folder containing the Private File text file should now exist (with Mike as owner) on the NTFS-formatted drive:

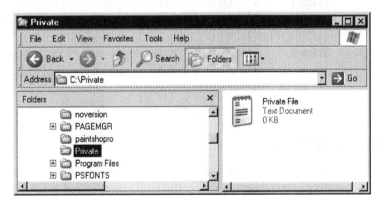

**Step 4.**   At the Properties dialog for the Private folder, go to the General tab. Click Advanced. Select the Encrypt Contents To Secure Data check box. Choose to encrypt all subfolders and files within the folder.

The Private folder, and all its files and subfolders should now be encrypted.

**Step 5.**   You should not be able to access the Private File text file while logged on as Administrator. The file has been encrypted, and you do not have the private key required to decrypt the file.

**Step 6.**   From the Administrative Tools menu, open the Certificates console. Expand to Certificates | Current User | Personal. Right-click the Personal folder and choose to Import. Once you supply the password (next step), you should be able to import into the Certificates console the certificate that you saved to the floppy disk in step 2.

**Step 7.**   After you have entered the password and completed the import of the certificate to the console, you should be able to access the Private File text file.

**Step 8.**   Right-click the Private folder, and select Properties from the pop-up menu. Click Advanced. Clear the Encrypt Contents To Secure Data check box. Click OK. The encryption attribute should be removed from the Private folder and from the Private File text file.

## Lab Solution 12.02

Managing local users and groups is a standard chore for an administrator. Here's how to go about it to meet the requirements of this lab.

**Step 1.**  The Computer Management administrative tool should be opened to show the Local Users and Groups objects.

**Step 2.**  The Dean, George, Keith, and Ali user accounts should be created in the Users folder. Each account should be configured with the specified password settings. The Supervisors and Staff group accounts should be created with the respective users. The Power Users built-in group should have the Dean and George user accounts added to the group.

**Step 3.**  You should be able to log on to the computer with each of the newly created user accounts. The Ali account should ask you to change the password at logon.

**Step 4.**  The George user account should have the ability to create other users accounts now that it has been added to the Power Users group.

## Lab Solution 12.03

The security policies that you were asked to create are typical for many installations of Windows XP Professional. Here's how you should have approached the task.

**Step 1.**  Click Start and then Run. Into the Run box, type **mmc**, and then click OK. At the MMC, add the Group Policy snap-in as directed

**Step 2.**  Expand Local Computer Policy | Computer Configuration | Windows Settings | Security Settings | Account Policies | Password Policy. The minimum password length should be configured to 7 characters in the Group Policy Console.

**Step 3.**  You should not be able to create the Tony user account with a password of 1234 at the Computer Management console:

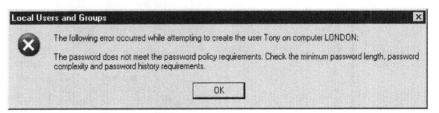

The password does not adhere to the new password policy settings that you just configured.

**Step 4.**   The Account Lockout Duration and Reset Account Lockout Times should change to the default time of 30 minutes once the Account Lockout Threshold is configured.

**Step 5.**   You should be locked out of the computer after three unsuccessful logon attempts using the Cathy account. The policy settings that you applied should lock out the account and force it to remain locked out for 30 minutes.

**Step 6.**   At the console, and expand Local Computer Policy | Computer Configuration | Windows Settings | Security Settings | Local Policies | Audit Policy. The Audit Policy should be selected.

**Step 7.**   You should have been able to configure the audit settings as instructed.

**Step 8.**   You should not be able to access the Accounting folder while logged on with the Dean user account. Your action should generate an event in the Security error log.

**Step 9.**   Success audits and failure audits should appear in the Security log of the Event Viewer administrative tool, indicating a successful logon of both the Dean and Administrator accounts, and the failed attempt to access the Accounting folder by the Dean user account. Here's a sample:

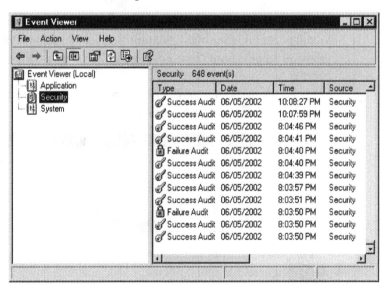

## Lab Solution 12.04

Making the necessary comparison and applying the template should be an easy task for you now that you're becoming so familiar with Windows XP Professional. Here's how you should proceed.

**Step 1.**   The Security Configuration and Analysis snap-in should now show in the console.

**Step 2.**   The security templates that are added to the console are

- **Setup Security**   The Setup Security template applies default computer settings during installation. Those settings include file permissions for the root of the system drive.

- **Compatws (Compatibility)**   The Compatws template provides default permissions for workstations and is primarily applied to Administrators, Power Users, and Users. The template makes certain that Administrators have the most power and that Users have the least. The Compatibility template is designed for Windows 2000/XP workstations only and should not be used on domain controllers.

- **Securedc and Securews (Secure domain controller and Secure workstation)** The Securedc and Securews templates should be applied to domain controllers and workstations. They define the security settings that are least likely to affect application compatibility. These templates also limit the use of LAN Manager and NTLM authentication protocols.

- **Hisecdc and Hisecws (Highly Secure)**   The Hisecdc and Hisecws templates are a superset of Securedc and Securews. It imposes further restrictions on encryption levels and signing. The settings for this template primarily affect domain controllers.

- **Rootsec (System Root Security)**   The Rootsec template specifies the new root permissions that were provided during setup. This template can be used to reapply root permissions, but it does not overwrite explicitly assigned permissions for the root.

**Step 3.**   With the hisecws template selected, click Open. Right-click the Security Configuration and Analysis object, and select Analyze Computer Now. Click OK to accept the default error log file name and path. The computer configuration should be analyzed in comparison to the hisecws template.

**Step 4.**   The results of the analysis should indicate that several settings in the current computer configuration are not up to the standards of the hisecws template. Red Xs will appear over settings that need to be changed if they are to match the hisecws template.

**Step 5.**   Right-click Security Configuration and Analysis, and select Configure Computer Now. Click OK. The hisecws template should be applied to the current computer configuration.

**Step 6.**   Right-click Security Configuration and Analysis, and select Analyze Computer Now. The computer configuration should again be analyzed. The new analysis should reflect the changes in the settings from your application of the hisecws template. All settings that needed to be upgraded have now been fixed.

**Step 7.**   By applying the Setup security template to the settings database, you have overwritten the hisecws template and brought the computer back to its default Setup security settings.

## ANSWERS TO LAB ANALYSIS TEST

1. The Encryption File System (EFS) can be implemented only on a drive that is formatted with the NTFS file system.

2. If you are running a Windows 2000 Active Directory forest, then you cannot implement Local Users and Groups on a domain controller. However, Local Users and Groups can be implemented on a Windows XP Professional computer in a domain environment.

3. To determine the rights that are granted to specific built-in groups, you can view the User Rights objects on the local computer. You can find the User Rights object at Local Computer Policy | Computer Configuration | Windows Settings | Security Settings | Local Policies | User Rights Assignment. When you make a user account a member of a built-in group, it inherits all user rights assigned to that group.

4. You can access the Security Template snap-in through the MMC, or by typing secedit.exe at the command prompt. The Security snap-in shows you all of the default security templates offered by Windows XP Professional. The templates are found in the *systemroot*\Security\Templates folder.

5. User accounts cannot contain the characters " ? ! \ [ ] : ; | = + *.

## ANSWERS TO KEY TERM QUIZ

1. Securedc template

2. Audit policy

3. Power Users

4. Cipher command line tool

5. recovery agent

MICROSOFT CERTIFIED SYSTEMS ENGINEER

# 13

# Monitoring and Optimizing System Performance and Reliability

## LAB EXERCISES

A
dministration of your Windows XP Professional computer requires that you not only create and manage users and data, but that you consistently monitor, manage, and optimize your system. Planning a sequence of common troubleshooting steps may be helpful and may save a great deal of time, because you can eliminate possible causes to problems one by one as you complete each step.

This chapter explores the issues of performance and data management so that you protect both user data and operating system data in the event of a failure. You will use the Performance console to monitor your system, the Backup tool to manage data, and the System object settings to optimize the performance of your computer.

**LAB EXERCISE 13.01**

# Monitoring the Windows XP Professional Computer

**30 Minutes**

Steve wants to monitor the current condition of his Windows XP Professional computer. He wants to learn more about the various monitoring components available to him in the Performance console. He would like to see the effects that a simple application has on his current system hardware. He would also like to have his computer alert him when disk space runs low.

## Learning Objectives

In this lab, you use the Performance console to monitor the Windows XP Professional computer. At the end of the lab, you'll be able to

- Identify the Performance console tools.
- Use the System Monitor to monitor computer activity.
- Analyze data to determine if bottlenecks exist.
- Create and configure a Performance alert.
- Trigger a Performance alert.

## Lab Materials and Setup

The materials you need for this lab are

- Pencil and paper
- Windows XP Professional computer

## Getting Down to Business

In this lab, you apply the knowledge that you acquired in the *MCSE Windows XP Professional Study Guide* by Curt Simmons (McGraw-Hill/Osborne, 2002) for monitoring a Windows XP Professional computer using the Performance console.

**Step 1.** Log on to the Windows XP Professional computer as Administrator. From the Administrative tools menu, open the Performance console. What tools are available for monitoring your computer?

_____

_____

**Step 2.** Select the System Monitor object. Notice the activity currently being monitored on your computer. What counters are monitored by default?

_____

_____

**Step 3.** Add these new counters to System Monitor: for the Processor object add the % Interrupts Time counter, and for the Physical Disk object, add the % Disk Time counter.

lab
ⓗint *The System Monitor appears with the counter activity evident in the chart view.*

**Step 4.** Note the current activity on your computer as shown in the chart. Open a new application on your computer, such as a game or the Calculator application. Use the application for a few seconds, and then return to System Monitor and note the activity as shown in the chart.

**Step 5.** Click the Freeze Display button on the toolbar. Analyze the counter data that is shown for each object. Are any bottlenecks evident?

_____

_____

**Step 6.** In the tree pane of the console, expand Performance Logs and Alerts. Create a new alert and name it **Free Space**.

**Step 7.** For the LogicalDisk object, add the % Free Space counter. Select the C: drive instance.

**Step 8.** Configure the alert to trigger when the value is under the limit of 80. Sample the data every 15 seconds. Choose the Action tab, and configure the alert to send a network message to your computer.

lab
ⓗint

*The value of 80 should trigger an alert on your system. You can alter the value if it fails to trigger the alert. For the purpose of this lab, we are using a high value, but in a real-life scenario, the value would be much lower.*

**Step 9.** At least one Messenger Service alert message should appear. View the message or messages, and click OK to close all boxes. Close the Performance console and log off the computer.

**LAB EXERCISE 13.02**

# Optimizing System Performance

**30 Minutes**

Edmund has been asked to analyze the performance settings of his Windows XP Professional computer. He needs to identify the various memory, processor, and appearance settings available for configuration so that he can determine the settings that will achieve optimal system performance. He has asked you to help him identify the appropriate objects and settings.

## Learning Objectives

In this lab, you optimize system performance on a Windows XP Professional computer. At the end of the lab, you'll be able to

■ Identify memory performance settings.

■ Identify processor performance settings.

■ Identify appearance settings.

■ Use the Task Manager to manage applications and processes.

## Lab Materials and Setup

The materials you need for this lab are

■ Pencil and paper

■ Windows XP Professional computer

## Getting Down to Business

In this lab, you apply the knowledge that you acquired in the *MCSE Windows XP Professional Study Guide* by Curt Simmons (McGraw-Hill/Osborne, 2002) for optimizing system performance on a Windows XP Professional computer.

**Step 1.** Log on to your Windows XP Professional computer as Administrator. Open the System object from the Control Panel and open the Performance settings.

**Step 2.** What is the function of the Visual Effects tab? What is the default setting for managing those visual effects?

_____

_____

**Step 3.** Select the Advanced tab. Under Virtual Memory, select Change. What do the Virtual memory settings on a computer indicate?

_____

_____

Close all open windows.

**Step 4.** Open Task Manager to the Applications tab. Open the Calculator application on your computer. Return to the Applications tab and ensure that the Calculator is listed with a status of Running.

**Step 5.** Select the Processes tab. Locate the calc.exe process and record the amount of memory that the application is using. Select the Applications tab, and end the Calculator task. Return to the Processes tab, and note that the calc.exe process has been removed. Close Task Manager, and log off the computer.

---

**LAB EXERCISE 13.03**

# Using Disk Defragmenter and Scheduled Tasks

**30 Minutes**

Krystin has noticed that her computer is slow in responding when she tries to open files. She wants to use the Disk Defragmenter tool to analyze the disk and then she wants to schedule drive defragmentation on a regular basis to resolve her problem.

## Learning Objectives

In this lab, you optimize system performance on a Windows XP Professional computer. At the end of the lab, you'll be able to

- Use Disk Defragmenter to analyze a disk.
- Use the Task Scheduler to schedule a disk defragmentation.
- Defragment a disk with a scheduled defragmentation task.

## Lab Materials and Setup

The materials you need for this lab are

- Pencil and paper
- Windows XP Professional computer

## Getting Down to Business

In this lab, you apply the knowledge that you acquired in the *MCSE Windows XP Professional Study Guide* by Curt Simmons (McGraw-Hill/Osborne, 2002) for scheduling tasks and using the Disk Defragmenter tool.

**Step 1.**   Log on to your computer as Administrator. At the Computer Management console, select Disk Defragmenter. Select your C: drive and analyze the drive to see if it needs to be defragmented.

lab
(h)int   *The analysis could take several minutes depending on the size of the disk drive.*

**Step 2.**   Once the analysis is complete, note in the space provided the percentage of fragmented files on the drive and the recommendation. Choose not to defragment the drive at this time. Minimize the Computer Management console.

_____

_____

**Step 3.**   Open the Scheduled Tasks console from the System Tools menu. Add a scheduled task to defragment the C: drive using the Disk Defragmenter program. If the Disk Defragmenter tools does not appear in the list of programs, you can browse to and find the defrag.exe tool in the /systemroot/windows/system32 folder.

**Step 4.**   Schedule the task to occur five minutes from the current date and time on your computer. Schedule the task to occur every two weeks at this indicated time. Ensure that you enter the correct Administrator password. Choose to view the Advanced properties of the task before completing the Scheduled Task wizard.

lab
(h)int   *The defrag property sheet should appear.*

**Step 5.**   At the Settings tab, configure to stop the task if it runs for six hours. Click OK. Wait a few minutes to ensure that the defragmentation task begins. Once the disk has been defragmented, delete the scheduled task from the Scheduled Tasks window, and log off the computer.

**LAB EXERCISE 13.04**

# Using the Backup Tool to Back Up and Restore Data

**45 Minutes**

Mitch is interested in using the Windows XP Professional Backup tool to back up his important files to a separate location in case of a system failure. He is concerned that the process of backing up and restoring data on his computer may be a difficult, and he has asked you to lead him through it.

## Learning Objectives

In this lab, you use the Backup tool to back up and restore data. At the end of the lab, you'll be able to

- Use the Backup wizard.
- Back up user data.
- Examine advanced backup options.
- Restore user data.

## Lab Materials and Setup

For this lab exercise, you'll need

- Pencil and paper
- Computer with Windows XP Professional installed
- Blank formatted floppy disk

## Getting Down to Business

In this lab, you apply the knowledge that you acquired in the *MCSE Windows XP Professional Study Guide* by Curt Simmons (McGraw-Hill/Osborne, 2002) for backing up and restoring data.

**Step 1.**   Log on to the Windows XP Professional computer as Administrator. Start the Backup tool. The Backup wizard opens. Clear the check box, so that the Backup tool does not open in wizard mode in future.

**Step 2.**   Choose to back up files and settings, and to specify the files that you want to back up. Expand My Computer, and select the System State object. What type of information is included in the System State Data object?

_____

_____

**Warning**   *Make sure to avoid selecting the check box for System State, because we will not be backing up that information in this lab. The System State check box should be clear.*

**Step 3.**   Expand the NTFS-formatted drive, and select the check box for the Management folder. Notice that the check box for the Private File.txt file is now also selected.

lab

**Hint**   *If you did not create the Management folder in a previous lab, use the Temp folder on your system drive instead.*

**Step 4.**   Choose to back up the selected folder and file to a blank floppy disk. Name the Backup file **Management**. Before you finish the wizard, select the Advanced button to specify additional backup options.

**Step 5.**   Choose to do a normal backup.
   What other options are available? Briefly list and describe each backup option in the space provided.

_____

_____

**Step 6.**   Choose to verify the data after backup, disable Volume Shadow Copy, and append the current backup to existing backups.

lab

**Hint**   *The Append or Replace options are useful when you are working with an existing backup. However, this is your first backup; those options don't apply in this lab scenario.*

**Step 7.**    Schedule the Management backup to run once, five minutes from your current computer time. Finish the wizard, and verify that the backup task shows in the Scheduled Tasks folder on your computer. Wait until the Backup completes successfully before moving to the next step. At Windows Explorer, delete the Management folder from the NTFS-formatted drive.

**Step 8.**    Again open the Backup tool from the System Tools folder. This time, the tool should appear as the Backup utility, rather than the Backup wizard. Select the Restore and Manage Media tab.

**Step 9.**    Browse to the location of the backup file on your floppy disk. Choose to restore the file to its original location, and start the restore. Once the restore is complete, choose to view the report. Ensure that your restore completed successfully. Close all open windows and log off the computer.

## LAB EXERCISE 13.05

# Examining the Recovery Console

**30 Minutes**

Dewi wants to examine the Recovery console that is available in Windows XP Professional. He has asked you to help him install the console on his computer and to identify the options and features of the console.

## Learning Objectives

In this lab, you install and examine the Recovery console. At the end of the lab, you'll be able to

- Install the Recovery console.
- Identify options for using the Recovery console.
- Examine the Recovery console features.

## Lab Materials and Setup

For this lab exercise, you'll need:

- Pencil and paper
- Windows XP Professional computer with 7MB free space and a CD drive
- Windows XP Professional CD

## Getting Down to Business

In this lab, you apply the knowledge that you acquired in the *MCSE Windows XP Professional Study Guide* by Curt Simmons (McGraw-Hill/Osborne, 2002) for installing and using the Recovery console.

**Step 1.**   Log on to the computer as Administrator. Insert the Windows XP Professional CD into your CD-ROM drive. Ignore the Windows XP window that may appear. At the Run command, type **D:\i386\winnt32.exe /cmdcons**, where D: is the letter of your CD-ROM drive.

**Step 2.**   Upon installation of the Recovery console, if you were to reboot your Windows XP Professional computer, you would see the Recovery console in the operating system selection menu. What is the advantage of installing the Recovery console on your Windows XP Professional computer, rather than simply running the console from the CD?

_____

_____

**Step 3.**   What other steps should you take before you attempt to use the Recovery console to recover a computer that is having problems?

_____

_____

**Step 4.**   What are some of the features of Recovery console in recovering a Windows XP Professional computer?

_____

_____

Log off the computer.

# LAB ANALYSIS TEST

1.  What differences exist between the Incremental and Differential backup types?

    _____

    _____

2.  What is the purpose of the Safe Mode feature of Windows XP Professional?

    _____

    _____

3.  What is the effect of setting the memory usage on the System object to optimize performance for programs?

    _____

    _____

4.  What views are available in the System Monitor component of the Performance console?

    _____

    _____

5.  What is the purpose of analyzing the disk drive with the Disk Defragmenter tool before starting the defragmentation process?

    _____

    _____

# KEY TERM QUIZ

Use the following vocabulary terms to complete the sentences below. Not all of the terms will be used.

Backup tool

baseline

bottleneck

Differential backup

disk defragmenter

Incremental backup

Performance console

Recovery console

Safe Mode

scheduled tasks

System Monitor

System Restore

system state data

virtual memory

1.  When monitoring your computer's activity, it is best to compare the data gathered with a _____ that was established when you computer was working correctly.

2.  When a component is not able to keep up with the demands placed on it, the problem is commonly called a(n) _____ .

3.  _____ allows Windows XP to use a portion of the computer's hard disk as a memory storage area.

4.  The collection of operating system data that includes the registry, COM+ class registrations, system boot files, and related information is called _____ .

5.  The _____ is a command-line tool that you can use to repair Windows XP Professional when it will not start.

## LAB WRAP-UP

Whether you're an experienced administrator or new to the tools that you've examined in this chapter, you should now be familiar with how to monitor a computer running Windows XP Professional. As well, you should be familiar with the tools that Windows XP Professional provides for optimizing system performance and for protecting user and system data in the event of a failure.

Congratulations! You have successfully completed all the labs in this manual. Take a moment to pat yourself on the back, and then rush right out to put the knowledge that you have acquired to good use on your Windows XP Professional computer.

# LAB SOLUTIONS FOR CHAPTER 13

In this section, you'll find solutions to the lab exercises, lab analysis test, and key term quiz.

## Lab Solution 13.01

To monitor a Windows XP Professional system and send network alerts to your computer, you should have completed the steps as described below.

**Step 1.**    Two Performance console tools are available for monitoring your system:

- **System Monitor**    The System Monitor charts real-time activity and displays information about the counters and objects that you choose to monitor.
- **Performance Logs and Alerts**    Performance Logs and Alerts records and logs server activity over a period of time. You can configure alerts to track activity and inform a user, start a process, or record the information to a log when a counter exceeds a defined threshold.

**Step 2.**    The Pages/sec, Average Disk Queue Length, and % Processor Time counters are added to the Performance console and monitored by default as shown in Figure 13-1.

| **FIGURE 13-1** |
|---|

Viewing the default counters in the System Monitor

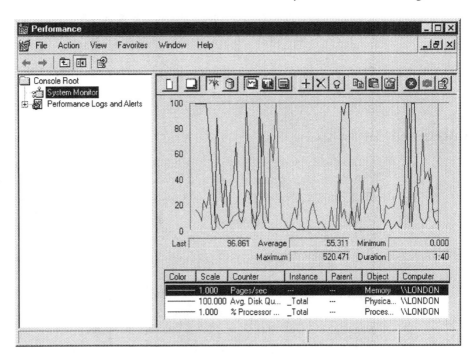

**Step 3.**   From the System Monitor toolbar, select the Add Counters button. In the Add Counters window, choose to add the specified counters. Click Close. The % Interrupt Time counter indicates the percentage of time that the processor spends receiving and servicing hardware interrupts. The % Disk Time counter indicates the percentage of time that a hard drive is reading or writing data.

**Step 4.**   System Monitor should have registered the new activity that you performed.

**Step 5.**   Answers will vary, but if your computer is performing well, opening a small application should not cause a bottleneck on your system.

**Step 6.**   Right-click Alerts, and choose New Alert Settings. Create the **Free Space** alert. Click OK.

**Step 7.**   You can add the % Free Space counter for the Physical Disk object to the alert from the General tab of the Alert dialog box. Monitor the C: drive instance.

**Step 8.**   You can set the alert threshold of 80 on the General tab of the Alert dialog box. Make sure that the interval is being sampled every 15 seconds. The Action tab is where you configure the alert to send a network message to your computer when triggered.

**Step 9.**   Alert messages should appear on your monitor screen once the alert is triggered.

## Lab Solution 13.02

To examine the settings for optimizing system performance on a Windows XP Professional computer, you should have completed the steps as described below.

**Step 1.**   To open the system performance settings, double-click the System object in the Control Panel. In the System dialog, choose the Advanced tab. Under Performance, click the Settings button.

**Step 2.**   Using the simple interface that Windows XP gives you in the Visual Settings tab, you can adjust the graphical nature of Windows XP to conserve RAM and processor cycles. The default setting on this tab lets Windows choose what's best for the computer.

**Step 3.**   Virtual memory allows Windows XP to use a portion of the computer's hard disk as a memory storage area. As data is loaded into memory and memory becomes low, pages of data are written to the hard disk. Those pages can then be recalled as needed. This feature allows Windows XP to keep more frequently accessed information readily accessible in physical memory, even when physical memory begins to run low.

**Step 4.**   Right-click the Taskbar, and select Task Manager. Select the Applications tab. After you open the Calculator, the Calculator application should show as Running on the Applications tab of the Task Manager.

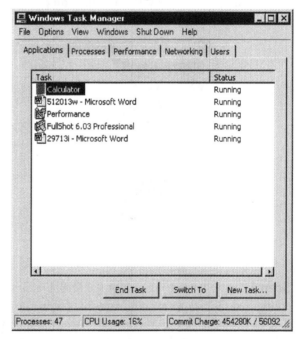

**Step 5.**   Answers will vary depending on how much memory the calc.exe process is using. Once the Calculator task has been ended, the calc.exe process is no longer visible on the Processes tab of the Task Manager.

## Lab Solution 13.03

To use the Disk Defragmenter tool and schedule a task on a Windows XP Professional computer, you should have completed the steps as described below.

**Step 1.**   Make sure to select the C: drive from the Disk Defragmenter tool. Click the Analyze button to start the disk analysis.

**Step 2.** Answers concerning the percentage of fragmentation on the selected disk drive will vary. Don't defragment the disk at this time, regardless of the recommendation received.

**Step 3.** The Scheduled Tasks wizard should have started when you selected Scheduled Tasks from the System Tools menu and chose to create a new task using the Disk Defragmenter (defrag) program.

**Step 4.** The time for the scheduled task will vary, but the task should be scheduled to occur every two weeks at the indicated time. Select the check box labeled Open Advanced Properties For This Task When I Click Finish. For example:

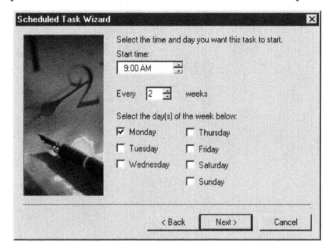

**Step 5.** On the Settings tab of the Disk Defragmenter task, you should have configured the task to stop if it runs for 6 hours, instead of the default 72 hours. The task should start up successfully. Afterward, remember to delete it from the Scheduled Tasks window.

## Lab Solution 13.04

To back up and restore data on a Windows XP Professional computer, you should have completed the steps as described below.

**Step 1.** To open the Backup tool, choose Backup from the System Tools folder.

**Step 2.** System State Data refers to a collection of operating system data, which includes the registry, COM+ class registrations, system boot files, and related information.

**Step 3.**   By selecting the check box for the Management folder, you automatically also select its contents—in this case, the Private File.txt file.

**Step 4.**   Make sure that you have chosen to back up the selected files to a floppy disk and specified the name Management for the backup file. You should have also selected to view the advanced options for backup.

**Step 5.**   You have selected the Normal backup option from among these available backup options:

- **Normal**   The Normal option backs up all selected files and marks them has having been backed up. All files that you select are backed up, regardless of their previously recorded backup state. This option is also known as a *full backup*. It is the type of backup that you initially use to back up data.
- **Copy**   The Copy option backs up selected files without marking them has having been backed up.
- **Incremental**   From among the selected files, the Incremental option backs up those that have changed since the last backup. This backup strategy reduces overall backup time and storage space. To restore, you have to recover the last Normal backup and every Incremental backup created since that Normal backup.
- **Differential**   From among the selected files, the Differential backup backs up those that are not marked as having been backed up. A differential backup may back up files that have not changed because they were not marked (as in a Copy or Daily). In the event of a failure, you need run only the Normal backup job for recovery with the Differential backup.
- **Daily**   The Daily option backs up all selected files that have changed during the day without marking them as having been backed up.

**Step 6.**   You should have chosen to append the current backup to an existing backup, even though that option does not apply in this lab scenario. You should have disabled the Volume Shadow Copy option from the advanced options of the wizard.

**Step 7.**   You should have successfully scheduled the backup to occur five minutes from the current time on your computer. The scheduled backup task should appear in your Scheduled Tasks folder. The backup task should then run successfully.

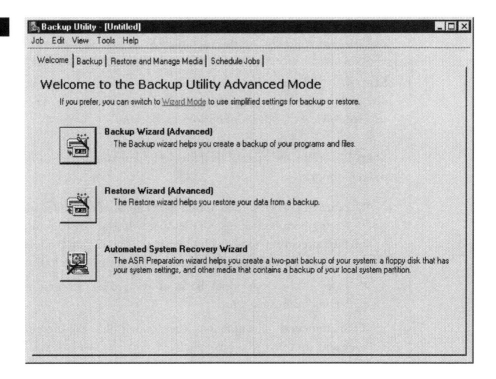

**Step 8.** Upon opening the Backup tool, you should discover that the tool now has a different view (Figure 13-2). You should have selected the Restore and Manage media tab.

**Step 9.** If you completed the restore process correctly, the report should indicate that the restore was a success.

## Lab Solution 13.05

To install and use the Recovery console on a Windows XP Professional computer, you should have completed the steps as described below.

**Step 1.** You should have successfully installed the Recovery console on your computer from the Windows XP Professional CD.

**Step 2.**  If you were unable to start your computer, you would most likely run the Recovery console from your setup CD. As an alternative, you can install the Recovery console on your computer to make it available in case you are unable to restart Windows. The advantage of installing the console is that you can then select the Recovery console option from the list of available operating systems on startup.

**Step 3.**  Before you attempt to recover a computer with Recovery console, you should try less intrusive methods, such as using Safe Mode and System Restore to solve startup problems.

**Step 4.**  With the Recovery console, you can access volumes on your hard disks and then start and stop services, access files and folders, repair the master boot record, and repair Windows XP Professional. You can even format drives.

## ANSWERS TO LAB ANALYSIS TEST

1. An Incremental backup backs up all selected files that have changed since the last backup. It takes less time and storage space than a Differential backup. In a Differential backup, all files that have changed since that last full backup are backed up.

2. Safe Mode enables you to boot Windows XP with a minimal number of drivers and a basic VGA interface. Safe Mode is useful when you are having problems starting Windows XP normally. Once the computer is booted into Safe Mode, you can begin to troubleshoot the system and resolve problems.

3. When the memory usage option is set to Programs, programs rather than system cache processes are given the most memory power. Depending on how much RAM you require, you can optimize memory for system cache if so desired.

4. The Chart, Report, and Histograms views are available in the System Monitor component of the Performance Console. Data can be viewed and saved using any of those formats.

5. Analyzing the disk drive provides a graphical display of the contiguous and fragmented files on the computer. It also notes any free space that may remain on the disk. After analysis, Windows XP Professional reports on the state of fragmentation and recommends defragmentation if necessary.

## ANSWERS TO KEY TERM QUIZ

1. baseline

2. bottleneck

3. virtual memory

4. system state data

5. Recovery console

# INDEX

/checkupgradeonly command line switch, 17, 24

## A

accessibility features, 54, 73
accessibility options, 46–48, 57–59
ACPI compliance, 85, 100
activation, product, 14
addresses, IP, 194–196, 204–205
administrator accounts, 52
alerts, 265
antivirus software, 17, 24
APIPA (automatic private IP addressing), 201, 211
application software, 12

## B

backing up data, 258–260, 262, 268–270, 272
BIOS, 122
Browsers
    Internet printer, 150, 160
    *See also* Internet Explorer
built-in groups, 240, 249

## C

callback options, 201, 211
/checkupgradeonly command line switch, 17, 24

clean installation, 11
client computers, 12
color profiles, 99
color quality settings, 83, 98
compatibility, 12
Compatws (Compatibility) template, 247
compliance, ACPI, 85, 100
compression, 139, 164, 175, 178–180, 191
configuring
    disks, 126–127
    fax support, 148–149, 156–159
    ICF (Internet Connection Firewall), 220–221, 227–228
    Internet Explorer, 214–216, 225
    keyboards, 102–103, 112–114
    language options, 50–51, 66–69
    local computer policies, 48–50, 60–66
    local printers, 142–143, 153–154
    local security policies, 236–238, 245–246
    mice, 102–103, 112–114
    modems, 104–105, 115–117
    offline files, 172–174, 188–190
    phone options, 104–105, 115–117
    power options, 81–82, 97–98
    Remote Desktop, 216–218, 226
    security, 166–168, 182–184
    TCP/IP, 194–196, 204–205
    Web Shares, 170–171, 185–188
    wireless links, 107–108, 118–121

# INTERNATIONAL CONTACT INFORMATION

## AUSTRALIA
McGraw-Hill Book Company Australia Pty. Ltd.
TEL +61-2-9417-9899
FAX +61-2-9417-5687
http://www.mcgraw-hill.com.au
books-it_sydney@mcgraw-hill.com

## CANADA
McGraw-Hill Ryerson Ltd.
TEL +905-430-5000
FAX +905-430-5020
http://www.mcgrawhill.ca

## GREECE, MIDDLE EAST, NORTHERN AFRICA
McGraw-Hill Hellas
TEL +30-1-656-0990-3-4
FAX +30-1-654-5525

## MEXICO (Also serving Latin America)
McGraw-Hill Interamericana Editores S.A. de C.V.
TEL +525-117-1583
FAX +525-117-1589
http://www.mcgraw-hill.com.mx
fernando_castellanos@mcgraw-hill.com

## SINGAPORE (Serving Asia)
McGraw-Hill Book Company
TEL +65-863-1580
FAX +65-862-3354
http://www.mcgraw-hill.com.sg
mghasia@mcgraw-hill.com

## SOUTH AFRICA
McGraw-Hill South Africa
TEL +27-11-622-7512
FAX +27-11-622-9045
robyn_swanepoel@mcgraw-hill.com

## UNITED KINGDOM & EUROPE
(Excluding Southern Europe)
McGraw-Hill Education Europe
TEL +44-1-628-502500
FAX +44-1-628-770224
http://www.mcgraw-hill.co.uk
computing_neurope@mcgraw-hill.com

## ALL OTHER INQUIRIES Contact:
Osborne/McGraw-Hill
TEL +1-510-549-6600
FAX +1-510-883-7600
http://www.osborne.com
omg_international@mcgraw-hill.com

www.ingramcontent.com/pod-product-compliance
Lightning Source LLC
Chambersburg PA
CBHW080355060326
40689CB00019B/4015